T0360473

Human Resource Management for Organisational Change

Change can take place in various forms, gradual or abrupt, incremental or transformational. It is a requirement in modern day society that everyone, whether at individual or organisational level, understands the softer nuances of this concept and prepares for it. During scenarios of change interventions, the role of human resources (HR) becomes crucial, even as the perception of it becomes ambivalent.

This volume delivers a holistic view on the role of HR in organisational change. It is built on the various theoretical models of change and provides a dramatic sequence of issues in change management to gain a big picture for HR managers and weaves through why, how and what perspectives to change management. *Human Resource Management for Organisational Change* offers a comprehensive coverage of the changing role of HR as it relates to organisational change theories and models, strategy, changing business environment and implications, organisational culture, leadership, resistance management, and high performance work practices (HPWP) to support change management and also gives an exposition of cost of no-changers. It is unique in that it covers the entire gamut of organisational change as well as HR.

It will be of value to researchers, academics, professionals, and students interested in learning more about how organisational change can improve productivity and human satisfaction as well as the systematic approach to managing organisational change.

Dr. Paritosh Mishra is Professor of Human Resources, Organisational Behaviour and Industrial Relations at Amity Business School, Amity University, Noida, Uttar Pradesh, India.

Dr. Balvinder Shukla is Vice Chancellor and Professor of Entrepreneurship and Leadership at Amity University, Noida, Uttar Pradesh, India.

Dr. R. Sujatha is Professor of HR and Entrepreneurship at Amity Business School, Amity University, Noida, Uttar Pradesh, India.

Routledge Focus on Business and Management

The fields of business and management have grown exponentially as areas of research and education. This growth presents challenges for readers trying to keep up with the latest important insights. *Routledge Focus on Business and Management* presents small books on big topics and how they intersect with the world of business research.

Individually, each title in the series provides coverage of a key academic topic, whilst collectively, the series forms a comprehensive collection across the business disciplines.

Optimal Spending on Cybersecurity Measures
Risk Management
Tara Kissoon

Small Business, Big Government and the Origins of Enterprise Policy
The UK Bolton Committee
Robert Wapshott and Oliver Mallett

Conflict, Power, and Organizational Change
Deborah A. Colwill

Human Resource Management for Organisational Change
Theoretical Formulations
Dr. Paritosh Mishra, Dr. Balvinder Shukla and Dr. R. Sujatha

Human Resource Management and the Implementation of Change
Dr. Paritosh Mishra, Dr. Balvinder Shukla and Dr. R. Sujatha

For more information about this series, please visit: www.routledge.com/
Routledge-Focus-on-Business-and-Management/book-series/FBM

Human Resource Management for Organisational Change
Theoretical Formulations

Dr. Paritosh Mishra
Dr. Balvinder Shukla and
Dr. R. Sujatha

Routledge
Taylor & Francis Group

NEW YORK AND LONDON

First published 2022
by Routledge
605 Third Avenue, New York, NY 10158

and by Routledge
2 Park Square, Milton Park, Abingdon, Oxon, OX14 4RN

*Routledge is an imprint of the Taylor & Francis Group,
an informa business*

Library of Congress Cataloging-in-Publication Data
Names: Mishra, Paritosh, 1962- author. | Shukla, Balvinder,
author. | Sujatha, R. (Independent researcher) author.
Title: Human resource management for organisational change :
theoretical formulations / Dr. Paritosh Mishra, Dr. Balvinder
Shukla and Dr. R. Sujatha.
Description: 1 Edition. | New York, NY : Routledge, 2022. |
Series: Routledge focus on business and management | Includes
bibliographical references and index.
Identifiers: LCCN 2021025966 (print) | LCCN 2021025967
(ebook) | ISBN 9781032042954 (hardback) | ISBN
9781032042978 (paperback) | ISBN 9781003191346 (ebook)
Subjects: LCSH: Personnel management. | Organizational
change.
Classification: LCC HF5549 .M5277 2022 (print) | LCC
HF5549 (ebook) | DDC 658.3--dc23
LC record available at https://lccn.loc.gov/2021025966
LC ebook record available at https://lccn.loc.gov/2021025967

ISBN: 978-1-032-04295-4 (hbk)
ISBN: 978-1-032-04297-8 (pbk)
ISBN: 978-1-003-19134-6 (ebk)

DOI: 10.4324/9781003191346

Typeset in Times New Roman
by MPS Limited, Dehradun

Contents

Acknowledgements

We start by acknowledging several people in many organisations with whom we have interacted over the last seven years while conceptualising and working on the various facets of this book. Their constant suggestions, prodding and evaluations have given direction to this book.

We wish to thank the reviewers who have painstakingly reviewed our draft versions by taking time out of their busy schedules and giving critical suggestions regarding improving the structure, content and format of the book. Only by complying with the hundreds of suggestions of the reviewers, could the book reach its current shape.

Our sincere thanks go to Amity University, Uttar Pradesh who have kindly consented to the publication of the book, which is carved out of research carried out at the University. We sincerely acknowledge the support and encouragement given by friends and colleagues during the endeavour to complete this book.

We acknowledge the support, co-operation and understanding of our family members extended to us during this period, without which this endeavour would not have come to fruition. Our love and thanks to Smruti, Suren and Ram, from the bottom of our hearts.

We also thank one another. We have learnt a lot through our process of research and writing a book together. Our variegated backgrounds propel us to look at things differently and from different perspectives. We debate, discuss, contend and air our views before we draw our conclusions, and this book is a culmination of such hours and hours of discussions. We hope to carry this forward and come out with more of such books for our readers.

Preface

A brilliant metaphor has been used by managerial guru Sumantra Ghoshal to describe corporate change in his DMA-Escorts award-winning book, Managing Radical Change, written in collaboration with Gita Piramal and Christopher A. Bartlett:

> From a caterpillar to a butterfly sounds and feels good! From an ugly, black caterpillar to a bright, colourful butterfly – the symbol of fantasy, of love, of good cheer! But imagine what is happening to the caterpillar as it goes through this metamorphosis. First it goes blind. Then its legs fall off. Finally, its body splits open, to allow the beautiful wings to emerge. Think of the fear and the pain it goes through. Which caterpillar, willingly and of its own volition, will sign up for the transformation?
>
> (Ghosal, Piramal & Bartlett, 2002, p. 50).

Then why should a caterpillar sign up to undergo this trauma? The answer is that perhaps it is a matter of compulsion, not of volition.

HR, being the function that inevitably is vested with inculcating the desired cultural change within the organisation, becomes one of crucial functions to transform and to bring about the organisational transformation on the journey of professionalism. In so far as HR function is to deal with and manage people, HR inevitably has important activities to perform whenever organisations need bring in change interventions. But who wants to change from an already existing comfort zone? It is said that only people who want to change are babies who have wet diapers. This book gives the readers an overview of what change is and how organisations can prepare for change management.

HR generally is considered a thankless profession. And more so by HR professionals themselves. HR is perceived as a function which receives more brickbats than bouquets. HR professionals feel that when the business is doing well, others take the limelight and when the palmy days are over for the business, HR bears the brunt. In good times, budgets are enough, and organisations comfortably spend on HR activities such as recruiting, training, rewards, employee engagement systems and the like. However, when the budgets are squeezed, HR becomes one of the first functions to get a knock down. During scenarios of change interventions, the perception towards HR becomes more ambivalent.

HR is a conduit between the management and employees. Sometimes in the process HR gets management-driven and the employees lose trust in it. And sometimes HR becomes too employee-oriented and management starts to look upon it with suspicion. It is an inevitable paradox that HR must balance.

The first author of the book has been an HR professional for more than three decades in Indian Public and Private Sector companies, as well as with a multi-national company. Having been instrumental in bringing in change interventions in a Maharatna Public Sector Undertaking, the biggest Private Sector Company in India, a relatively small Promoter driven Company and a large American Multinational Company, this aspect of HR function has always been intriguing. More so, because sometimes the changes brought in have been revolutionary in nature. This intrigue propelled the first author to research this aspect in great details.

This research programme stretched over more than five years between 2014 till 2019. This book "Human Resource Management for Organisational Change: Theoretical Formulations" deals with the theoretical foundations of Change and HR's role in it.

Dr. Paritosh Mishra
Dr. Balvinder Shukla, and
Dr. R. Sujatha

Introduction

Change happens in society in various forms – gradual or abrupt, incremental or transformational. It is a requirement in modern day society that everyone, whether at individual or organisational level, understands the softer nuances of this concept and prepares for it. The "boiling frog" is a beautiful metaphor that cautions people to be cognizant of even slow, but steady changes, lest they should ultimately suffer unwanted consequences. If a frog is put abruptly into a pot of boiling water, it will jump out; if the frog is put in normal water, which is subsequently boiled slowly, it will not feel the accelerating heat and will be boiled to death. On the other hand, there is the other metaphor of describing transformation – that of an ugly, black caterpillar changing into a bright, colourful butterfly. This is a change that is inherently fraught with fear and pain, but finally results in a symbol of beauty, colour, love and romanticism.

This is an age in which all organisations are subjected to fundamental changes. Almost all postulates about managerial practices are being questioned. The old methods no longer work well enough, and this necessitates a fundamental redefinition of managerial principles.

Theoretical Foundation

Historically, industrial prosperity has been built on the exploitation and exhaustion of natural resources. However, of late, technological advances and upsurges in global developments are challenging the very genesis of that economy. Rather than material resources or physical assets, knowledge as a resource is now considered the new foundation of wealth and source of competitive advantage. In order to leverage knowledge assets, however, organisations must alter the way they organise and use human resources. Hence, organisations must transform fundamentally the way they organise, operate and use human

DOI: 10.4324/9781003191346-101

resources as the ultimate tool for succeeding in the market. This book builds the theoretical foundations of a research problem: Does the maximisation of potential of human resources and employees lead to organisational success in modern day business and industrial systems?

In the incessant journey towards success and excellence, every organisation at some stage does its own soul-searching and launches itself in the trajectory of growth and expansion. How does it come about? Is it an automated, unconscious process? Rather, is it a consciously maneuvered process? What are the HR systems that interact to bring about such change? What is the role of Human Resources in bringing in organisational change? Is HR a cause for organisational change or is it a victim of the change process? What is the role of Leadership in bringing about change? In this book, the authors grapple with the issues of the role of the human resource function in the organisational change process of companies, the level of effectiveness of the human resource systems to sustain organisational change, and the degree of integration between the organisational structure and the human resource strategy for change management.

This book builds theoretical foundations on organisational strategy, implications of changing business environments for the changing role of HR, models of organisational change, resistance to change, interface of organisational culture and leadership with organisational change, role of HR in change and resistance management, and high performance work practices (HPWP) to support change management. The authors elaborate on the conceptual dimensions with an eye on examining the role of human resource function in the organisational change process of companies, the level of effectiveness of the human resource systems to sustain the organisational change, degree of integration between the organisational structure and the human resource strategy for change management, and the like.

Conceptual Framework

A conceptual framework for the detailed study of a Research Problem is built up, which is shown in Figure 0.1.

The organisational change paradigm consists of several political, economic, social, technological, environmental and legal factors. The change paradigm also draws on organisational strategy, culture, leadership and its styles and several psychological and behavioural dimensions. HR strategy and structure are both offshoots of organisational paradigm, as well as its influencer. Further, HR creates various High Performing Work Practices, such as Performance Management Systems, Competency

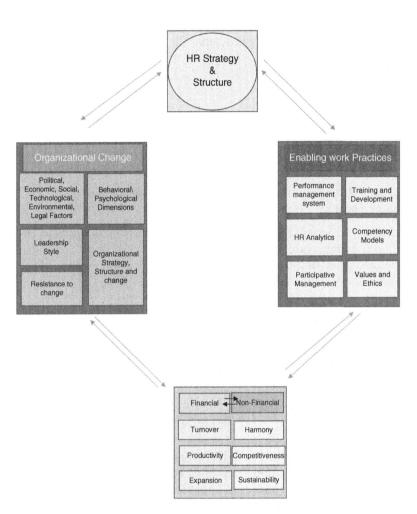

Figure 0.1 Conceptual framework for examining the role of hr in organisational change.

models, HR Analytics, Participatory processes and Value-based and ethical systems. The organisational processes and HR strategy mutually influence one another, and the result is organisational change, manifest through financial performance such as increased turnover, productivity and expansion of business. Other non-financial indicators like harmony, competitiveness and sustainability also result. Further, the financial and non-financial parameters influence one another.

A Tour of the Book

The layout of the book is given herewith.

Introduction

This chapter lays the foundation of the book by explaining all elements of the book in brief. For this study, the introduction covers the issues the authors grapple with, and gives a conceptual framework of the Research Problem and the structure of layout of the book.

Chapter 1: Organisational Strategy and Changing Business Environment

Chapter 1 theorises that organisational Strategy and business environment influence each other dialectically. This chapter deals with the models of Business strategy and factors impacting change in the business environment and their impact on HR.

Chapter 2: Changing Role of Human Resource Management

Chapter 2 deals with evolution of the HR function from Personnel Management to Human Resource Management, to Human Capital Management, and further on to Change Management.

Chapter 3: Organisational Change

Chapter 3 defines organisational change and classifies change based on its scale or timing, and whether it is brought about by economic value (Theory E) or organisational capability (Theory O). This chapter also discusses various approaches to Organisational Change and analyses organisational change vis-a-vis organisational metaphors.

Chapter 4: Models of Organisational Change

Chapter 4 investigates a few famous models postulated by management analysts, such as Kurt Lewin's Three Step Model, John Kotter's Eight Step Model, Nadler and Tushman's Congruence Model and Peter Senge's Systemic View.

Chapter 5: Resistance to Change

Chapter 5 deals with the theories on resistance to change, including psychological and behavioural dimensions, and examines the causes for resistance.

Chapter 6: Organisational Culture and Organisational Change

Chapter 6 deals with issues of organisational culture and organisational change, including cultural adaptation and change management through cross-cultural dimensions.

Chapter 7: Leadership and Organisational Change

Chapter 7 deals with roles of leaders vis-à-vis organisational Change Metaphors as well as divergent leadership styles.

Chapter 8: Human Resources and Organisational Change

Chapter 8 deals with some theoretical formulations on role of HR in Change management, including some tools on how the Human Resource Department can help individuals and organisations sail through change smoothly. Some aspects, such as formulation of change management plan, crystallisation and actualisation of the change vision, preparation and implementation of a communication matrix and rewards and recognition Strategy and role in resistance management, are specifically examined in this chapter.

Chapter 9: High Performance Work Practices (HPWPs) to Support Change Management

Quite often Companies build HPWPs to improve operational efficiency and organisational performance and support change management. This chapter makes an exposition of a few of such HPWPs, such as performance management and feedback mechanisms, building competencies and training and development, HR analytics, participation of employees in decision making process, and value-based and ethical systems.

Conclusions

This book is written keeping in mind the needs of multiple segments of users. Advanced undergraduate students and master's students will find this book useful as a reference, as it gives a succinct but comprehensive coverage of the subject. For Doctoral and Post-doctoral students and other researchers, this book provides a very good prologue to the field. As a Research book, it provides an comprehensive list of references that will give researchers a solid overview of the topic. Business leaders and HR practitioners looking for solutions to their change management problems may also find the book useful, as it has been written with an eye to examine the role of the human resource function in the organisational change process of companies, the level of effectiveness of the human resource systems to sustain the organisational change, the degree of integration between the organisational strategy and the human resource function.

1 Organisational Strategy and Changing Business Environment

Organisational Strategy, business environment and Human Resources have a triangularly impacted relationship – each influencing the other dialectically. This chapter depicts the models of business strategy and changing business environment and their impact on Human Resource Management.

Organisational Strategy

The term strategy is derived from the Greek word, strategos. Originally the term was used in the military parlance. However, "businesspeople have always liked military analogies, so it is not surprising that they have embraced the notion of strategy" (Essentials, 2005, p. xii). Strategy is a "plan that aims to give the enterprise a competitive advantage over rivals through differentiation" (Essentials, 2005, p. xiv). It is a plan, as suggested by Porter (1998, p. 73), focused on "positioning ... [and] operational effectiveness". According to Porter, strategy is the creation of a unique and valuable position, involving a different set of activities. Thus, Strategy involves a common thread of logic that links policies and resources together into a coherent and consistent whole (Andrews, 1971; Ansoff, 1965).

Strategic management characterises an academic turf, where consensual meaning of strategy may not be feasible. Asking strategic management scholars to describe the field could result in divergent responses (Nag, Hambrick, & Chen, 2007). Despite the seeming discordance, Nag et al. (2007) believe that the connotation still has a consensual identity, even as there may be some obscurity about its formal definition.

Nag et al., (2007) espouse an academic definition of strategy which they believe incorporates all the relevant elements of the construct. Their definition (Nag et al., 2007, p. 944) is: "The field of strategic management

DOI: 10.4324/9781003191346-1

deals with the major intended and emergent initiatives taken by general managers on behalf of owners, involving utilisation of resources, to enhance performance of firms in their external environments".

According to Ketchen (2003, p. 95) strategic management deals with three levels of strategy. Strategy at the corporate level dwells on the answers to the question "In what industry or industries will we compete?" Business-level strategy answers the question "How will we compete in each of our chosen businesses?" The task of functional-level strategy is to explore "How will each of the organisation's functional areas support our business and corporate level strategies?"

Changing Business Environment

Several factors, internal and external, working in unison, affect organisational strategy. Selznick (2011) has introduced the need to bring an organisation's 'internal state' and 'external expectations' together for creating goals and plans.

External force can be understood as the factors that influence the organisation from outside, such as dynamic changes in technology, society, market environment, and politics (Joseph, 2013). These forces have the capacity to bring changes in the production process, management relations, nature of competition, organisational methods, etc. Among external forces, technology plays a vital role in modern organisations, since it determines the entire structural working. Equally important are the market conditions, since the rise and fall of the market affects the success of the organisation (Joseph, 2013).

Internal factors are mainly concerned with changes brought about in the organisation by internal organisational elements. Internal changes can occur from implementation of new technology, changes in the behaviour of the workforce, decline in performance of the employees, merger and acquisitions of departments and induction of new employees, among other factors. (Armstrong, 2006; Durai, 2010; Lientz & Rea, 2004). Many a time, technological change brings turbulence in the organisation (Collins, 2005). Employees need to get attuned to the changing technological skills to maintain their jobs and status.

Internal changes are also experienced by the organisation when the workforce or employees change their attitude towards work (Collins, 2005; Lientz & Rea, 2004). This can happen due to change in working environment, changes in skillsets, or onset of negativism.

Internal changes are also encountered when new employees are hired, inducted and managed. The Michigan School of thought put this as the human resource cycle, consisting of four conceptual functions performed by every company: selection (or recruitment process); appraisal; rewards; and development (Armstrong, 2006). The efficacy of these functions determines whether the employees will bring development, growth, and change to the organisation.

Several Models have been conceptualised by managerial thinkers to study strategy making in organisations. It is expedient to study a few such models.

The Six-Box Model

Marvin Weisbord (1976), has espoused a diagnostic model, popularly known as the Six-Box Model. It seeks to capture all essential features of organisational performance determinants that can help organisations adapt to change (Palmer, 2005).

In the context of organisational life, Weisbord (1976) suggests six broad categories for organisational diagnosis: Purpose; Structure; Relationship; Rewards; Helpful mechanisms; and Leadership. The Model is described herewith.

The Six-Box Model represents the interaction between internal organisational structure and external environment, with 'Purpose, Structure, Relationship, Rewards, Helpful mechanisms and Leadership' representing internal organisation structures. These structures impact one another dialectically as inputs and outputs (Rothwell, 2013), and in turn are encircled by the broader external environment. As a diagnostic tool, this model cautions that giving too much emphasis to only one box of internal structure while ignoring the others or concentrating too much on the internal structures while not giving attention to the external mileau, brings downfall of the organisation. All the variables overlap with one another, helping and diagnosing problems when necessary, and thus ultimately condition organisational progress and development. According to this model, if the organisation faces problems, questions need to be asked with respect to each internal variable to diagnose the gap and find solutions (Rothwell, 2013; Weisbord, 1976).

Weisbord (1976) Model has remained a good organisational diagnostic framework often adapted by researchers (e.g., Hamid, Ali, S. S., Reza, Arash, Ali, N. H., & Azizollah, 2011; Ihsani & Syuhada, 2020; Lok & Crawford, 2000).

Strengths, Weaknesses, Opportunities, and Threats (SWOT)

The origin of the term "SWOT" is not clear. Wikis credit SWOT's origination to Stanford University Professor Albert Humphrey, but no academic reference to support this claim is available (King, 2004). Haberberg (2000) states SWOT is an idea initially used by Harvard academics in the 1960s, while Turner (2002) credits SWOT to Ansoff (1987). SWOT analysis links the firm's capability to its pertinent competitive environment. It focuses on assessing the strategic position of a firm by analysing its strengths, weaknesses, opportunities and threats (Jobber, 2004).

SWOT analysis assists in identification of environmental relationships as well as development of suitable growth paths for organisations (Proctor, 1992). Valentin (2001) observes that SWOT analysis is the traditional means for looking into ways of designing and maintaining a profitable fit between a commercial venture and its environment. It is one of the most respected, often used and prevalent tools of strategic planning (Glaister & Falshaw, 1999; Omer, 2019).

Porter's Diamond Model

The concept of competitive advantage epitomizes the key element of the strategy definition developed by Porter (1985). Porter espouses that competitive advantage is "at the heart of a firm's performance in competitive markets" (Porter, 1985, p. XV) and "grows fundamentally out of the value a firm is able to create for its buyers that exceeds the firm's cost of creating it" (Porter, 1985, p. 3).

Firms quite often do an assessment of their competitive advantage vis-à-vis the external environment based on the five forces model (Porter, 1980, 1985). The 'five forces' of competitive position of Porter's diamond model, which is a simple framework for measuring and evaluating the competitive strength and position of a commercial organisation, has been viewed as the major analytical framework of competitive positioning paradigm.

Porter defines the competitiveness of a market as the productivity that companies located there can achieve (Cairncross, 2001). There are five forces that regulate such competitive strength and appeal. Porter's five forces help ascertain where power lies in a business scenario and can be suitably leveraged not only in identifying the strength of an organisation's extant competitive position, but the strength of a scenario that an organisation may aspire to move into. The five forces under consideration are: threat of new entrants or their barriers to entry; bargaining power of suppliers; threat of substitute products and services; bargaining power of buyers; and rivalry among competitors (Porter, 1985).

Porter's model has certain limitations. It presupposes a characteristically perfect market and a stationary market structure, which are seldom found in today's uncertain world. Further, some industries are intricate, having manifold interrelationships. This makes Porter's model difficult and incomprehensible to be used (Wang, 2004). Moreover, as Rumelt (1991) points out, the critical factors of profitability are often firm-specific rather than industry-specific. Prahalad and Hamel (1990) suggest that resource-based competitive advantage, rather than one based purely on products and market-positioning, is more significant and sustainable.

VRIO Framework

'VRIO framework', initiated by Barney (1991), represents a counterbalance for the method centred on external causality related to firm's competitiveness. VRIO (value-rarity-imitability organisation) technique (Barney, 2002) has assumed wide-spread advocacy for assessing a firm's resources. In this framework, strategic assets are Valuable (economically significant, i.e., these make money for the company), Rare (unique, i.e., few other companies may have these resources), Inimitable (unmatched, meaning that it would be expensive to duplicate them and tough to ascertain what practices other companies are adopting to have such strategic assets), and have Organisational Support (strong management support and processes and systems to back these assets).

Such Resource Based View (RBV) is criticised for focusing solely on internal resources, ignoring the nature of market demand (Hooley et al., 1996). Andrews (1971) and Chandler (1962) have contended that external and internal factors cannot be dissociated. Maier and Remus (2002, p. 107) bring out the conceptualisation of fit, as a fine balance between Market Based View (MBV) and RBV. Dyer and Singh (1998) as well as Wang (2004) espouse that in the interconnection between the firm and the environment is embedded the obtaining of competitive advantage. Nason and Wiklund (2018) advocate versatility in resources and argue that valuable, rare, inimitable and non-substitutable (VRIN) resources support firms to exploit unique opportunities, while versatile resources bring in novelties in recombining the resources of the firms to promote growth.

PESTEL Framework

The success or failure of an organisation is determined by the level of efficacy of interaction with its environment. Kotler and Armstrong (2004) state that various kinds of limitations are imposed on organisations by the environment. An environmental analysis should categorize important external factors that require organisational action. Several frameworks exist to carry out environmental analysis; however, Johnson, Scholes, and Whittington (2008) prefer the PESTEL framework, which classifies factors into political, economic, social, technological, environmental and legal. The PESTEL framework, which is a mnemonic for the factors just enumerated, groups macro-environment factors for assisting strategists to look for sources of general opportunity and risks (Witcher & Chau 2010, p. 91).

Political Factors

Political factors include government regulations with which organisations must comply, in addition to possible changes in governmental regimes leading to policy changes. Even though changes in Government policies affect almost all nuances of business, all businesses are not affected equally by such changes. This is because of divergent political strategies adopted by different business firms. Managers adopt three different business responses to public policies – passive reaction, positive anticipation or proactive public policy shaping (Weidenbaum, 1980). Research has shown that business firms which are active politically tend to be larger, have a more international scope and are in more heavily-regulated industries (Zardkoohi, 1985).

Economic Factors

Economic factors include cost-related matters for the organisation (Witcher & Chau, 2010), and may consist of changes in public spending, interest or exchange rates, or the climate for business investment. Rosman, Shah, Hussain, and Hussain (2013) emphasise the importance of a nation's economy on Human Resource policies. In the same manner, Mello (2006) points out that organisations should predict the future of the economy and plan their functions.

The most important economic factor affecting business during modern times has been globalisation and the emergence and growth of Multi-National Corporations. Businesses have now come to accept that 'globalisation of product and services' as well as 'globalised talent markets' have changed the way business is conducted (Leung, Bhagat, Buchan, Erez, & Gibson, 2005).

The study of cross-cultural dimensions in MNCs has assumed prominence for two reasons. First, MNCs apply the mechanisms of coordination in the process of centralisation, formalisation and socialisation across business functions, (Bartlett & Ghoshal, 2002) and second, considering the responsiveness of local governmental regimes (Bartlett & Ghoshal, 2002), many MNCs have started operations and sharing of knowledge jointly with the units in the host countries.

The impact on HRM practices found across countries (Budhwar & Sparrow, 2002) and in foreign subsidiaries and joint ventures (Bjorkman & Lu, 2001; Ferner & Quantanilla, 1998; Rosenzweig & Nohria, 1994) has been a topic of interest for Management researchers. MNC's subsidiaries and JVs are influenced both by institutional factors in the host country and by international isomorphic processes, such as downward pressures from the MNC parent company (Westney, 1993). Cultural-cognitive and normative institutional processes prevalent in the host country play significant roles in HRM practices in situations of uncertainty (DiMaggio & Powell, 1983; Levitt & March, 1988). It has been reported (Braun & Warner, 2002) that the HRM practices in units where the MNC holds a minority share are more locally adapted than those in foreign wholly-owned and majority-owned units. Farley, Hoenig, and Yang (2004) found several significant differences in HRM practices between foreign subsidiaries and joint ventures. The background of the HR manager is likely to influence the effects of isomorphic pulls. An HR manager recruited from a local organisation is more likely to perceive local companies as the reference point and this is likely to affect the kind of practices suggested and implemented in the unit (Shenkar & Zeira, 1987). Research suggests that the role played by the HR department in the diffusion process generally is more strategic in Western corporations than in Chinese and Indian firms (Budhwar, Luthar, & Bhatnagar, 2006; Child, 1994; Cooke, 2004).

Social Factors

Social factors relate to lifestyles, attitudes, buying habits or demographic changes, and may also relate to culture within the organisation, including the usage of social media, which has been influencing business management and activities in a big way (Daley, 2010). Zvirbule and Vilka (2012, pp. 44–46) have identified the importance of socio-economic factors, such as demographic patterns, size of population, population growth rate, family size, age composition, beliefs and values, tastes and preferences and education. There is general agreement among experts that the effect of socio-cultural elements on the personality and behaviour of people in India is very strong (Shivani, Mukherjee, & Sharan, 2006). Lloyd and Duffy (1995) believe that families are becoming more dispersed. The diminishing ability of men to earn a family wage, coupled with the growing need for cash for family maintenance, has caused an increasing number of females to engage in economic activities (Lloyd & Duffy, 1995). There has been an increase in female-headed households, which could be due to a variety of reasons, such as widowhood, migration, non-marital fertility and marital instability (Bruce & Lloyd, 1992).

Technological Factors

The business environment has changed drastically recently because of various forms of technology-propelled disruption. Some of them are explained herewith:

Digitalisation

As per the Moore's law, postulated by Gordon Moore, co-founder of Intel, the performance of computing technology such as the microchip doubles its levels of capacity and speed every 18 months or so. This can correspondingly be made applicable to other technologies such as robotics, nanotechnology, 3D printers and the like. Where does this lead us? Some authors of science fiction, such as Arthur Koestler or Karel Capek and Isaac Asimov have wondered that the ultimate tool of human beings seems to be another human being. Would that mean that the scientists' technological inspiration would be to create something as humankind's mirror image, or in other words to play God? Or just to procreate a child?

Digitalisation implies connecting technology, data science, devices, design and business strategy to change a business process or customer experience. In fact, there are several ways the new technologies are changing the contours of business and value chains, some of which are detailed herewith:

i. **Electronic Deliverability:** Some products can be delivered electronically more easily than others. For example, it is far easier for an Aviation Company to enable its customers to book tickets online and deliver the same via e-mails than for an automobile company to deliver its products.

ii. **Information Intensity:** Even as all products and services have some information to be showcased and presented to the customers, the quantum of it varies. For example, automobiles have volumes of operating guidelines, whereas smaller items like cakes come with few details. In the past, it was cumbersome to collect information about products. Customers had to take the trouble of searching the data they required by visiting the vendors and reading the manuals or other available documents. The Web has enabled companies to provide easily the desired information content about products and services.

iii. *Customizability:* IT enablement helps customize information, suited to the requirements of specific customer segments. Even as customisation may help sophisticated items such as laptops or computers, it may not be of great help in the case of small products such as home appliances.

iv. *Aggregation Effects:* Products and services can be aggregated or joined in different ways. In earlier days, customers dealt with a bank for their savings, another for foreign exchange, an insurance agent for life and automobile policies and an independent financial adviser for their long-term investments. Thanks to deregulation and modern technology, banks can offer a portfolio of bundled services to meet all those financial needs through a single account.

v. *Search Costs:* Nowadays, the Web provides customers with a plethora of information, regardless of their location or time zone. Further, such information is made available in real time in any manner the customer may want. This helps reduce the costs of search. Also, now technology has brought in more transparency in transactions. Both customers and suppliers can these days compare specifications, prices and service attributes. Take, for example, the aviation industry. A buyer can easily compare prices of different airlines and pick up the one that best serves the needs. However, such transformation of the market is not achieved with respect to other low-value products. Say, for example, a waist belt, whose features, such as colour, quality or thickness is limited and is mostly constant.

vi. *Real-Time Interface:* This is essential for businesses and customers who require information that remains in flux and volatile. A good example is online trading. For instance, customers value human touch, but human touch alone is now unable to reach the people, and many customers find it more convenient to speak to or interact with machines most of the time (Westerman & Bonnet, 2015).

Digital technologies are transforming the business landscape, offering tremendous opportunities to companies for venturing into new ways of working. The world is now filled with apps, social media, analytics and the cloud, and many tech-savvy companies are transforming the way they conduct their business, as digital technology offers business the opportunities to transform the way they are networked and managed (Westerman & Bonnet, 2015), instead of just confining them to traditional and conventional business logic (Kurti & Haftor, 2015). NTPC, the 'Maharatna' Public Sector Undertaking in India, forayed into paperless office in May 2017, with the objectives of optimal utilisation of the office space, smooth retrieval of office records and promotion of clean and green office environment (Digital initiatives, 2017). The Automotive and Farm Equipment Business of Mahindra and Mahindra, a USD 19.4 billion multinational group based out of Mumbai, India, has devised a game-based application, Farmathon, for Mahindra employees, which enables users to have knowledge of different aspects of farming and can provide innovative ideas to help improve farming practice (Mahindra, Great Place to Work, 2019).

ERP

Competition, expansive markets and mounting expectations from customers in today's business world, increase the pressure on organisations to reduce costs, curtail throughput times, bring down inventories, diversify product choice, stick to delivery dates with unfailing accuracy, improve quality and harmonise global demands, supply and production (Shankarnarayanan, 2000). There is a demand for organisations to integrate all business processes. The workplace is going through intense changes consequent upon technological disruptions and emergence of novel organisational forms, which affect people as to where and how they work (Bleecker, 1994; Dambra & Potter, 1999; Davidow & Malone, 1992; Wang, Liu, & Parker, 2020); Yager, 1997). Ushering in of technology provides new roles and opportunities for Human Resource Management, even as it helps other departments to embrace technology. During recent times, the phenomenon of the virtual workplace has gained currency. It describes how Information Technology is used to generate networks of people interacting in different ways, fettered neither by time nor space (Crandall & Wallace, 1997, 1999).

Several software options are now available in the market, but only a few allow interaction among various systems. Further, many of them cannot be customised. Hence, they are not of help to optimize the organisational business processes. Enterprise Resource Planning (ERP) is a leading software which helps integrate all departments and processes, viz. manufacturing, marketing, quality control, sales, supply chain management, inventory and other areas in the company in a solitary computer system and integrate all of them in one single database. It is an integrated, configurable and customizable package that is suitable to fast-changing business needs (Davenport, 1998).

ERP provides two major benefits that exist in integrated departmental systems: (1) an integrated holistic view of the business enveloping all segments; and (2) a Company database, where all business transactions are passed in, recorded, processed, checked and reported. This holistic view increases collaboration and harmonisation of all functions, departments and segments. It also allows enterprises to achieve augmented communication and responsiveness to diverse stakeholders. ERP provides competitive advantage through better control and superior visibility of information. It brings robust change leading to innovation and smart decision-making (Chung, 2007).

Artificial Intelligence (AI)

Businesses are now increasingly affected by Artificial Intelligence (AI) systems that can recognize speech or images or analyze patterns of online behaviour. AI has come to be envisaged in super-smart humanoid robot form that can process big data and accomplish a range of mundane tasks more effectively than human beings (McLellan, 2015). In recent years, the AI revolution is headed by such successful companies as Google, Microsoft, Amazon, and Facebook, among others (McLellan, 2015). Within organisations, business intelligence has always been there, but exponential growth in technology capabilities, smarter analytics engines and the surge in data, which are mostly initiated by AI, have simply transformed the way organisations conduct their business. In business, the explosive growth of complex and time-sensitive data generates decisions that give organisations competitive advantage. Sectors such as health care, financial services, and travel have revolutionised the way they conduct their business by taking recourse to AI (McLellan, 2015; Power, 2015). Among business organisations, IBM is leading the integration of AI in industry (Power, 2015). A range of digital technologies such as bioacoustics sensing, biochips, machine learning, quantum computing, smart robots, and other virtual technologies transform the AI system, which in turn influence business. AI has been subsuming business intelligence and other digital related services easily, because it has large amounts of processing power and can speed up the work at rapid rate (McLellan, 2015).

Uberisation

Uberisation is one manifestation of the revolution technology has brought about in the workplace (Bhatt, 2015). Digitalisation puts information directly in the hands of stakeholders simultaneously and thus changes many managerial dimensions such as capacity deployment, supplier-choice and the visibility of customer satisfaction. Uber, the ride sharing company, which originated out of an endeavour to reduce the efforts for locating a cab on the streets of San Francisco, today operates in almost 65 countries and more than 700 cities.

> In the third quarter of 2014, Uber accounted for 3% of business travellers' incidental expenses … Just one quarter later, that share expanded to 5%. As a percentage of total taxi rides, Uber usage has tripled from 11% in January 2014 to 33% of January 2015.
>
> ("Expenses Uber", 2015)

As of 2020, 15 million uber trips are completed each day globally, with 91 million monthly active users globally, and over 22,000 employees (Srivastav, 2019). Many other businesses have used the Uber model, including medical services for non-emergency cases and legal support.

Internet of Things

The term internet of things (IoT) refers to scenarios where network connectivity and computing capability extends to physical devices, vehicles, buildings, sensors and everyday items not normally considered computers, allowing these systems and objects to generate, collect, exchange and consume data with minimal human intervention. Internet of Things allows smarter products to be produced and smarter businesses to be operated and greatly influences the changing business firmament (Marr, 2015). It helps businesses make things bigger, much bigger, and smarter to operate and be successful. The Internet of Things is the constantly increasing world of sensors and devices that create a plethora of granular data about everyday activities. As the quantum and diversity of sensors and other telemetry sources grow, the inter-connections between them and the related analytics also grow to create an IoT value curve that is rising umpteen number of times as time goes on. This upward trend in IoT value will continue as capacity and performance of sensors and embedded computers grow in harmony with Moore's law and economics.

Telematics

Telematics is the branch of science concerned with the use of technological devices to transmit information over long distances (Telematics, 2021). It helps in providing information required by business. For instance, through telematics, business activities such as procuring materials, selling products and giving services are conducted with ease (Antonelli, 2012). This is because telematics provides faster service. In India, while in 2014, 2G was the main network of connection, subsequently by 2016, 3G and 4G networks were ushered in. 5G networks, which provide greater bandwidth and faster data downloads, thus helping speed up the way business is conducted, is likely to be operational in India in the second half of 2021 (Explained: What is 5G, 2021). Upgrading to faster networks means that more data can be downloaded, and business can expand without much investment on networking. Telematic also means integrating smartphones and tablets in conducting daily business work. Through telematics, many business organisations have also integrated 'Application Programming Interface' (API) that allows third party software to be integrated, giving business a wider network. This third-party software allows telematics data to be integrated into back-office systems or ERP systems to improve workflows and operational analysis.

Drones

Wikipedia defines drone or 'an unmanned aerial vehicle (UAV) as 'an aircraft without a human pilot aboard' (Unmanned aerial vehicle, 2019). Drones, which constitute the bad boys of the Internet of Things, are no longer known as being used for spying, but are being used to help in meeting various business needs. For instance, real estate industry has been revolutionising the business through the usage of drones, which help in inspecting the sites quickly, safely and efficiently (Lawson, 2016).

Cloud Technologies

According to Investopedia, 'Cloud computing is a method for delivering information technology (IT) services in which resources are retrieved from the Internet through web-based tools and applications, as opposed to a direct connection to a server' (Cloud computing, 2021). While cloud technologies are not exactly new technologies, in recent years, this system has been transforming business models, and the efficiency of these models has also increased. Cloud computing gives employees easier access to organisational working since this allows them even to work from home, with the ability to access mail, documents, and other data related to work. It also allows employees and organisations not to be worried about storage capacity, thus making organisations less concerned about investing more capital expense for storage (Goodenough, 2013). Cloud computing is also accelerating, in what has come to be commonly known as, the 'Bring Your Own Device' (BYOD) trend, that allows employees to virtually 'dial into' their corporate systems with their own systems, like computers or tablets (Goodenough, 2013; Lawson 2016). This system therefore allows employees and business organisations to work without having the threat of crashing the infrastructure they use. Some companies which have adopted BYOD and the culture of flexible and mobile working are Cyxtera, an infrastructure company providing a global data centre platform with advanced cybersecurity, Ivanti, a provider of IT management solutions, LastPass, a provider of password-management system, 3CX, a provider of cloud-based unified communications platform, Trustonic, a provider of hardware security systems which purportedly are used in 1.5 billion devices worldwide (Em360, 2018).

Impact of Technological Changes

Companies are leveraging human capital technologies for use by everyone in business. E-HRM (Electronic-Human Resource Management), the 'digital workplace' and the 'digital employee experience' are all concepts emerging as HR mega trends. E-HRM is a web-based solution that takes advantage of the latest web application technology to deliver an online real-time Human Resource Management Solution (Gowan, 2001). Noe, Hollenbeck, Gerhart, and Wright (2000) define e-HRM as the processing and transmission of digitised information used in HRM, including text, sound, and visual images, from one computer to another electronic device. Today devices of all kinds are coming online and getting interconnected in networks at lightning speed, but for all the potential and possible success, it is essential that the right analytic architectures are in place. True for HR systems as well. Such systems allows human analytics to provide an organisation with insights in effectively managing employees so that business goals can be realised efficiently and effectively (Edwards & Edwards, 2016).

Cisco Systems India Pvt. Ltd., which is the world leader in networking for the internet, has introduced a machine learning powered search, christened Belong, for its talent acquisition purposes, which brings out the most relevant candidates and predicts their openness to Cisco opportunities (CISCO, Great Place to Work, 2019). Tata Communications uses AI-based algorithm to show only a 'Masked Resume' where identifiers related to gender, such as name, email, photo, and pronouns are masked, and only the skills, qualifications and experience of the candidate are seen by the hiring managers. This helps eliminate gender bias during the screening stage while hiring (Tata Communications, Great Place to Work, 2019). Novac Technology Solutions Pvt. Ltd., the IT and ITES arm of Shriram Value Services, which provides domain expertise in finance, retail, mobility, and e-learning solutions, proffers Learning Management System, which caters to customised, gamified and scenario-based learning. The objective of the LMS, MyCoach, is to provide a dynamic and high-end learning support for skill development and personal and professional growth, leading to integrated growth of the employees and the organisation (Novac, Great Place to Work, 2020).

In the contemporary world, virtual desktops have grown in popularity among businesses because of the need to increase their employees' productivity levels through such system. This productivity through a virtual desktop can be initiated by enabling organisations to accept it as business policies, and letting employees to use it in roaming, to access the same applications or information from different locations and places. This will improve customer service and give limitless environment for bringing change and development. Business process as a service (BPaaS) is especially relevant for small and medium enterprises, helping them in such cases where they cannot afford to have fully-fledged enterprise solutions (Yu, Zhu, Guo Huang, & Su, 2015). It presents a service where there is penetration of the cloud model in the business process that goes beyond the conventional IT service. It is the combination of business process with cloud services that monitors the activities and feedback of organisations. Through BPaaS, the traditional activities of business process management systems are uploaded to the cloud service which help assess business process and operations (Stammer & Wilson, 2013). This system gives customers flexibility and advantage in connecting with organisational business system.

Results Only Work Environment (ROWE), as a human resource management strategy shaped by Jody Thompson and Cali Ressler, shows that employees should be paid only for their output and not for the hours invested. Many companies have started to adopt such ROWE, as it reduces the workday strategy as well as increases employees' productivity. Companies like 'Best Buy' effectively implement such policies (Hitt, Ireland, & Hoskisson, 2009). It makes employees to gain more ownership of their work and express greater satisfaction with ROWE.

Many essentials of the digital employee profile intersect with the employees' digital work and home experiences. The lines of demarcation of the two profiles are becoming increasingly fuzzy. Posting on Facebook, buying vacation tickets through Yatra or planning a marriage anniversary party by getting ideas on Google might all dwell in the realms of the digital home experience. However, taking work home to create a presentation on a home computer or using an online tool for the same would be considered as a crossover. In view of these overlaps of the digital work and home environments, it is important for HR to approach the concept of creating a formal digital work experience with both environments in view.

Environmental Factors

With growing sensitivity toward environmental issues, companies are taking bigger responsibility for making sustainable development a reality. Many Companies are proactively taking green HR interventions. NTPC has launched the Samvaad app in 2019, which is a customised smartphone application to revamp its internal communications and is available for download on Playstore and iOS. It is used for sharing of news, events and achievements of the organisation and its employees and provides information in 17 languages (NTPC Internal Communications, 2019).

To assimilate sustainability into business strategies, there must be a quantifiable link between environmental actions and financial performance. Epstein and Roy (2003) have proposed a framework that could assist managers making the business case for sustainability initiatives. Within the context of that framework, they have scrutinised a sample of corporate sustainability reports to (1) determine whether companies have been measuring the fiscal impact of environmental initiatives, (2) identify specific areas of concern and difficulties for the integration of sustainability into corporate performance and (3) provide specific guidance on how companies can have a better integration of environmental and social initiatives in their decision-making processes. The results reflect that companies are increasingly attempting to link environmental initiatives to financial performance.

Roscoe, Subramanian, Jabbour, and Chong (2019) examine the relationship between Green Human Resource Management (GHRM) practices, the enablers of green organisational culture, and a firm's environmental performance, explaining that the enablers of green organisational culture positively mediate the relationship between GHRM practices and environmental performance.

Legal Factors

This includes existing or new legislation, such as the introduction of changes in the minimum wages or changes in Health and Safety legislation. This is examined in three different dimensions:

Legal Regime and HR

Policies for human resource management need to be in consonance with legal necessities. Law is the basis of HRM practices and policies. According to Tiwari and Saxena (2012), HRM practices need to be adapted to the regulations of countries. Hence, the differences of HRM practices also depend on such legislation and regulations. Kane and Palmer (1995) have observed that equal opportunity, occupational health, and industrial relations can be influenced primarily by the legislation of the country. Mello (2006) aver that, legislation and regulation influence every function of an organisation, so, too the human resource management decisions. Similarly, Mabey and Salaman (1995) identify the importance of government policies and legislation on strategic training and development activities.

In India, the employment laws were crafted immediately after independence when the primary concern of legislature was protecting and ameliorating the conditions and interests of the working class. In 2020, Government of India has promulgated four labour Codes such as Codes on Wages, Industrial Relations, Social Security and Welfare, and Occupational Safety, Health and Working Conditions by combining and abridging the provisions of the existing 44 central labour laws. This action is aimed at reducing the complexity of compliance, promoting a conducive business environment and enabling the ease of doing business. This is also expected to improve life and livelihood and the working conditions of workers. Despite hurdles, the Government of India expects to bring the Codes into operation expeditiously.

Notice of Change

Even as in today's world of competition change has become an inexorable necessity, the legal regime in India quite often makes change a difficult process. For example, any sort of change requires a prior notice of 21 days and compliance to processes as laid down in Section 9A of Industrial Disputes Act, 1947. No change can be made effective in respect of any item listed in the Fourth Schedule of the Industrial Disputes Act, 1947 without such notice of change. The Fourth Schedule lists the following circumstances which require notice of change:

i. Wages, including the period and mode of payment;
ii. Contribution paid, or payable, by the employer to any provident fund or pension fund or for the benefit of workers under any law for the time being in force;
iii. Compensatory and other allowances;
iv. Hours of work and rest intervals; leave with wages and holidays;
v. Starting, alteration or discontinuance of shift working otherwise than in accordance with standing orders;
vi. Classification by grades;
vii. Withdrawal of any customary concession or privilege or change in usage;
viii. Introduction of new rules of discipline, or alteration of existing rules, except in so far as they are provided in standing orders;
ix. Rationalisation, standardisation, or improvement of plant or technique which is likely to lead to retrenchment of workers;
x. Any increase or reduction (other than casual) in the number of persons employed or to be employed in any occupation, process, department, or shift, not occasioned by circumstances over which the employer has no control.

These appear all-pervasive. Further, change in a Unionised environment becomes even more difficult, as the moment there is a notice of change, Unions can raise an industrial dispute leading to Notice of Conciliation by the Conciliation Officer. Further, under Section 33(1) (a) of the Industrial Disputes Act, 1947, during the pendency of any conciliation proceeding before a conciliation officer, no employer shall alter, to the prejudice of the workmen concerned in the industrial dispute, the conditions of service applicable to them immediately before the commencement of such proceeding. This essentially means that prior to giving notice of change, the employer must mandatorily enter into a settlement either under Section 12(3) or under Section 18(1) of the Industrial Disputes Act, 1947. Further, in a multi-union environment, a settlement under Section 18(1) of the Industrial Disputes Act, 1947 is applicable only to such workmen who subscribe to such settlement in writing.

Outsourcing

Despite the rigidities of the laws, it would be interesting to see how entrepreneurial leadership and strategy formulation can leverage the opportunities represented by the gaps between what the law says and what the market needs (Waiting Line, Outlook Business, 2010). Sometimes entrepreneurs see 'an opportunity to build a business on the transmission losses between how the law is written, interpreted, practiced and enforced' (Sabharwal, 2008, as cited in Khanna & Raina, 2010). The entire outsourcing industry in India is built on such 'transmission losses'.

In India, the hiring of temporary workers is subject to the proviso in The Contract Labour Prohibition and Abolition Act (1970) and Industrial Disputes Act, 1947. Outsourced Jobs and services which are carried out within the premises of the principal employer are covered under the Contract Labour (R&A) Act. Under Section 10 in the Contract Labour (Regulation and Abolition) Act, 1970, the appropriate Government, after satisfying itself as to whether a process, operation or other work is incidental to, or necessary for the industry or whether it is of perennial nature, whether it is done ordinarily through regular workmen in that establishment or an establishment similar thereto, may prohibit the employment of contract labour. In both the Contract Labour Regulation and Abolition Act, 1970 and Industrial Disputes Act, 1947, the principle of vesting a right for permanence after working for specified number of days (viz. 240 and 120, respectively) is immanent.

Even as the liberalisation of the Indian economy in the wake of 1991 created enormous job opportunities, it unravelled the stark truth of growing shortage of skilled manpower in India. Identifying, hiring and onboarding employess having the right skillsets emerged as a challenge. Against this backdrop, 'temping' or temporary employment services (temp markets) emerged as a new phenomenon to bridge this gap in employability. The opportunities that emerged were connecting demand for skillsets and prospective candidates with its supply of jobs, training of candidates in soft skills and computer literacy for bridging the short-term gaps between employability and availability and long-term investment for building the pipeline of talent through quality education.

Internationally, the temp market was over a $140 billion industry by 2002. However, in India temping was non-existent in the organised formal sector. The option for the entrepreneurs was to wait for the laws to change, or to grab the opportunities as they emerged. However, structural constraints do not impede the right opportunities to evolve. As Sabharwal, one of the founders of Team Lease clarified, 'In India the noise to signal ratio is very high and you should focus on the signal'... and further, 'The Industrial Disputes Act and the CLRA obstruct the fundamental right to work. I am breaking the law because I am doing good' (as cited in Khanna & Raina, 2010).

The Indian temp outsourcing industry was worth INR 270 billion in 2015 and it is growing 12% year on year (Vyas, 2016). The outsourcing industry is expected to grow exponentially in India, propelled by the digital transformation exercises in the country.

Concluding Observations

Traditional approaches to strategy assumed that there is relative stability in the world and strategic interventions have relatively predictable results. As has been observed, however, several factors, such as globalisation, technology, and changes in societal norms, converge to make the business environment volatile and uncertain. Several models on organisational strategy making have been theorised by management thinkers. Some of these models have been around for a longer period than others. There is no rough and ready answer to the question, 'Is one model is superior to the other?' Nor can any cut and dried solution be proffered by any model. These models have been used in various case studies in several ways. Further, management practitioners have also used the models based on their understanding of which one applies most to their organisation's way of thinking. However, there is no gainsaying that the strategic model adopted by the organisation does affect all functional aspects in the organisation, including its Human Resource Management.

2 Changing Role of Human Resource Management

Management is the art and science of managing the organisational resources, viz. financial resources, information resources, physical resources, and human resources (Griffin, 2006). Thus, human capital is one among the four kinds of assets being managed in an organisation (Adeniji & Osibanjo, 2012), the other three being physical, financial, and intangible assets. All such assets are indispensable to the functioning of an organisation; however, human assets constitute the fulcrum around which all other operations revolve. According to Du Plessis (2009), an organisation's workforce is its sine qua non and represents one of its most powerful and treasured resources. The functionalism regarding Human Resource Management has undergone changes and has evolved through the vicissitudes of time.

From Personnel Management to Human Resource Management

Workforce management in its rudimentary nuances started in England in the later Middle ages along with the systems of craftsmen and apprenticeship and further got institutionalised with the ushering in of the Industrial Revolution in the late 1800s. Frederick Taylor, in the 19th century, focused on labour productivity, while simultaneously espousing equitable systems of rewards for improved productivity. Later, several factors, such as sweeping changes in technology, progress of organisations, enlargement of unions and governments' concerns and interventions in welfare of workers, converged to usher in the development of personnel departments in the 1920s. Personnel administrators were then being called 'welfare secretaries' (Ivancevich, 2007).

The phrase 'Personnel Management' emerged in Management literature after World War II in 1945. Traditionally, the role of Personnel Management, in addition to salary payments and training, was to 'hire

DOI: 10.4324/9781003191346-2

and fire' personnel in organisations. The focus of 'Personnel management' was the accomplishment of administrative tasks, such as record keeping, administration of wages, salaries and benefits, looking after labour relations, viz., complications with trade unions or problems emerging in employer-employee relationships.

The term Human Resource Management has gradually replaced the term Personnel Management (Lloyd & Rawlinson, 1992). The growth of the Human Resource function, which historically has also been associated with the progress of business (Conner & Ulrich, 1996; Walker, 1999), has experienced a revolution, having been changed from the traditional administrative role to a bigger one encompassing both human resource management and corporate strategy in unison (Barney & Wright, 1998). Whereas some researchers have held that human resource management is the central concept that connects the management of employees in an organisation to the business and its external milieu (Truss & Gratton, 1994), others have averred that the concept has evolved into a channel between business strategy and human resource management functions (Butler, Ferris, & Napier, 1991; Glaister, Karacay, Demirbag, & Tatoglu, 2018; Lengnick-Hall & Lengnick-Hall, 1988; Lorange & Murphy, 1984; Szierbowski-Seibel, 2018).

Personnel management, in the traditional sense, is undergoing its biggest ever change, including having been rechristened as human resource management (Rimanoczy & Pearson, 2010). However, Armstrong (2000) contends that the alteration in nomenclature is immaterial; what is of greater significance is the ushering in of new people practices and HRM policies to meet the requirements of the day. Armstrong (2009) describes Human Resource Management (HRM) of an organisation as a strategic approach to managing the employees, who individually and collectively work towards the attainment of organisational objectives. Storey (1992) observes that HRM through its systems brings in HR philosophies, strategies, policies, processes, practices and programmes, in a systematised and coherent manner.

Human Capital Management

In modern times, organisations expect the HR function to transcend the role of mere provisioning of transactional personnel and administrative services and focus on providing mechanisms to leverage on human capital (Jamrog & Overholt, 2004). Pfeffer (1994) describes how changing market conditions renders many of the traditional sources of competitive advantage, such as patents, economies of scale, access to capital, and market regulation, less important than the core competencies (Hamel & Prahalad, 1994) and capabilities (Stalk, Evans, & Shulman, 1992) of employees, that help develop new products, deliver world class customer service, and implement organisational strategy. Albeit such forms of intellectual or organisational capital (Tomer, 1987) are largely invisible (Itami, 1987), the sources of such capital are not, as they rivet on a capable, inspired and adaptable work force, and in the Human Resource Management system that develops and sustains it. Hamel and Prahalad (1994, p. 232) argue that these 'people embodied skills' are directly reflected in conventional measures of firm profitability.

Research on integration of Human Capital Management and business strategies has attracted a lot of attention in the history of research on managerial science (Brockbank, 1999; Delery & Doty, 1996; Devanna, Fombrun, & Tichy, 1984; Golden & Ramanujam, 1985; Martell & Carroll, 1995; Truss & Gratton, 1994; Wright & McMahan, 1992; Zula & Chermack, 2007). The research on role of HR in value co-creation has accordingly evolved (Baird & Meshoulam, 1988). There has also been ample work on how Strategic HR ushers in competitive advantage (Barney, 1986, 1991, 1992; Boon, Eckardt, Lepak, & Boselie, 2018; Colbert, 2004; Conner, 1991; Crook, Todd, Combs, Woehr, & Ketchen Jr, 2011; Fey, Bjo"rkman & Pavlovskaya, 2000; Grant & Baden-Fuller, 1995; Inyang, 2010; Reed & DeFillippi, 1990; Schuler & Jackson, 1987; Walker & Stopper, 2000; Wright & McMahan, 1992). Many experts contend that the human resource function must promote practices, which would augment employee performance, not only at the individual level, but at the organisational level, as well (Garavan, Costine, & Heraty, 1995). Thus, HRM functions in current times significantly focus on contributing to organisational performance and corporate strategy (Barney & Wright, 1998). In fact, HR has moved a long way from being saddled with a vortex of criticism and plethora of questions regarding its validity, which subsequently resulted in a cornucopia of research that had found a nexus between HR practices and organisational performance (Stewart & Woods, 1996).

HRM as Change Management

In the contemporary business world, competition is pronounced, customer expectancy is high and there is extreme paucity of time to develop and market new products and services (Yukl, 2008). "To respond to the pace of change, organizations are adopting flatter, more agile structures and more empowering team-oriented cultures" (Piderit, 2000), "using change agents, empowerment, prepare people for change, help people deal with stress" (Deal, 1985), "building innovative and learning organizations, building a broad coalition" (Denis, Lamothe, & Langley, 2001), "keep people informed and demonstrate optimism...to implement change" (Yukl, 2008) and using and mastering human resources information systems (HRIS) in enhancing organisational agility (Marhraoui & El Manouar, 2020).

Many have looked at HRM to provide a conceptual framework for the organisations' leadership teams to better manage crisis situations at the institutional level (Radulescu & Ioan, 2009; Wang, Hutchins, & Garavan, 2009) and HRM specialists have increasingly been perceived as frontrunners of change (Du Plessis, 2009; Raeder, 2019; Rennie, 2003; Walker & Stopper, 2000).

Different segments of organisational population can play the role of bringing in change in an organisation – the CEO, a dedicated Change Management team to manage change, external consultants, line managers or HR Professionals (Thornhill, Lewis, Millmore, & Saunders, 2000). However, since any change initiative impacts people, the Human Resources function has an important role to play in change management. HRM is advantageously placed to play an active role in change management and achieve a strategic contribution (Caldwell, 2003), by replacing "resistance with resolve, planning with results, and fear of change with excitement about its possibilities" (Ulrich, 1997, p. 152).

When HR functions as 'change makers' (Storey, 1992), HR professionals are contributing to the fruition of change intervention by fulfilling different functional roles (Baran, Filipkowski, & Stockwell, 2019), which could be, for example, to provide the requisite resources (Thornhill et al., 2000, p. 26), help identify the process for managing change (Ulrich, 1997), or support the organisation in the process of institutionalisation of the changes (Ulrich, 1997). Using a broad range of HRM practices and executing them with care produces helpful results during times of change (Raeder, 2019). "HR professionals as change agents do not carry out change, but they must be able to get the change done" (Ulrich, 1997, p. 161).

Concluding Observations

Strategic Human Resources management has progressively highlighted that pre-emptive management of change supports organisations to subsist in a complex, volatile competitive and globalised business environment (Grieves, 2003). According to Nel et al. (2011), organisations that can manage change pre-emptively, can also unceasingly adjust their strategies, systems, bureaucracies, products and cultures to the changing requirements of time.

3 Organisational Change

Over the years, organisational changes in strategy, structure, systems and practices have been of immense interest to researchers and practitioners. Various kinds of literature have emerged in the area of change. A variety of perspectives on organisational change or transformation has been built over the years (Pettigrew, 1985; Wilson, 1992). This chapter attempts to define and classify organisational change and also discusses the various approaches to organisational change.

Defining Organisational Change

According to Burnes (2004), change is a ubiquitous feature of organisational life, both at operational and strategic level. Many organisational events are commonly christened as change, such as restructuring, downsizing, mergers and acquisitions, strategic change, cultural change and the like. Change is defined as "an empirical observation of difference in form, quality, or state over time in an organisational entity" (Van de Ven & Poole, 1995, p. 512). organisational change refers to the adoption of an idea, procedure, process, or behaviour, that is new to an organisation (Pierce & Delbecq, 1977).

Over time, a common verbiage for categorising organisational change has been established, including change that is incremental or transformative (Mohrman, 1989; Nadler, 1988), first-order or second order (Bartunek & Moch, 1987; Nadler & Tushman, 1995), transformational, transitional or transactional (Ackerman, 1986; Burke, 1994), and episodic or continuous (Weick & Quinn, 1999). These terms normally pertain to the scale, scope, or degree of change or whether the change has been just apparent or fundamental.

Another way in which change has been categorised pertains to the cause of change. The two major types here are change that stems from the impetus of internal or external factors. Nadler and Tushman

DOI: 10.4324/9781003191346-3

(1995) brand the former anticipatory and the latter reactive. Such categorisation differentiates between types of change that spring from inner, developmental forces and those that are brought about due to the need for organisations to adapt to external stimuli. There is a consensus that change, irrespective of being triggered by internal or external factors, comes in all shapes, forms and sizes (Balogun & Hope Hailey, 2004; Burnes, 2004; Carnall, 2003; Kotter, 1996; Luecke, 2003; Odor, 2018), and, therefore, affects all organisations in all industries.

Depending on the degree of change, Ackerman (1984) and Burke (1994) have characterised change process as transformational, transitional or transactional. Some researchers have further refined the categorisation of change process into finer distinctions. For instance, Flamholtz and Randle (1998) differentiate among three types of transformational change. **Type 1** epitomises the transition from an entrepreneurial to a formal organisational structure; **Type 2** implies the regeneration of a prevailing business; and **Type 3** constitutes an essential re-thinking on what industry or business the organisation is in. Such continuum of the scale of change is also treated by Neal and Tromley (1995).

Classifying Organisational Change

Based on the scale of change, Todnem By (2005) classifies change into four types: fine-tuning; incremental adjustment; modular transformation; and corporate transformation.

Fine-tuning describes change occurring at divisional or departmental level as in a continuing course corresponding to the organisation's strategy, processes, people, and structure. The rationale for fine tuning is to facilitate growth of employees commensurate to the organisational requirements and create instruments to augment volume by giving due consideration to cost and quality and through improvement of policies, methods and procedures (Dunphy & Stace, 1993). Further, fine-tuning fosters commitment, both at individual and group levels, to the organisational goals and mission and helps clarify roles and responsibilities and promotes confidence in the organisational values for facilitating excellence of departmental functioning (Dunphy & Stace, 1993).

Incremental adjustment encompasses discrete alterations in the managerial systems and processes and changes in organisational strategies; however, it does not comprise radical change (Todnem By, 2005). Modular transformation is change characterised by identifiable alterations in singular or several departments or divisions and is different from incremental adjustment in so far as it is radical, even if it concentrates on one part, as distinguished from the whole, of the organisation (Todnem By, 2005). Corporate transformation is, as the nomenclature signifies, company-wide change and is marked by radical changes in the business strategy of the organisations (Dunphy & Stace, 1993).

Approaches to Organisational Change

Hard and Soft Approach. Based on the approach adopted to identify change, it is categorised as brought about either by economic value (Theory E) or organisational capability (Theory O) (Beer & Nohria, 2000). Strategies for bringing in change under theory E categories are generally considered the hard approaches to change, characterised by substantial usage of monetary inducements, sweeping sackings, layoffs and restructuring. Corporate success is solely measured by augmentation of shareholder value. On the other hand, strategies for bringing in change under theory O categories are generally the soft approaches to change, achieved through culture building measures such as bringing about desired changes in employee behaviour, attitude, competences and commitment. Most organisations do not rely on either Theory E or Theory O in exclusivity, rather use both in combination and in varying degrees (Beer & Nohria, 2000).

Each of the two managerial theories, theories E and O, try to resolve the issue of change from two diametrically opposite perspectives. Theory E focuses on maximising shareholder value, managing change through top-down leadership approach, emphasis on structure and systems, motivation through financial Incentives. Theory O focuses on developing organisational capabilities, encouraging participation from the bottom, and building corporate culture and employee commitment through equitable use of compensation (Beer & Nohria, 2000, p. 137). Both endorse some managerial purposes, albeit with some intended or unintended costs. The managerial challenge is to reconcile the gap between the two theories and reap the benefit of each, while removing the negative fallout from each. However, there is no gainsaying that a combined approach must be sequential – Theory E tactics first, to be trailed by Theory O approaches.

Revolutionary versus Evolutionary Approach. Depending on the timing of change, organisational changes are categorised into two types – revolutionary and evolutionary.

Revolutionary change occurs through organisational command. Quite often such change occurs as a sequel to a change in leadership, or in situations of organisational crisis. For example, a new Chief Information Officer may come in and restructure the department, or the process of change may set in pursuant to failure of an IT department in an audit. On a more strategic plane, entrepreneurs often create some corrective mechanisms when an Organisation shows poor performance, or its existence is threatened. In fact, most of the observable endogenous changes in organisations are credited as deliberate panacea for fiascos and flaws. This presupposes room for entrepreneurial discretion (Fransman, 1999), which eventually results in organisational changes, revolutionary in nature.

Nelson and Winter (1982) have emphasised the evolutionary approach and contend that organisations quite often depend on routines to accomplish coordination. There are several variants of the evolutionary approach of organisational change and these are elaborated in the succeeding portions in this chapter.

A group of managerial thinkers categorise change as **situational improvisations**. Change is grounded in the continuing performances of organisational actors, and emerges out of their explicit or tacit, manoeuvrings and experimentations, in response to everyday exigencies, emergencies, interruptions, exceptions, threats and opportunities. March (1981, p. 564) notes,

> Because of the magnitude of some changes in organisations, we are inclined to look for comparably dramatic explanations for change, but the search for drama may often be a mistake…Change takes place because most of the time most people in an organisation do about what they are supposed to do; that is, they are intelligently attentive to their environments and their jobs.

Barley (1988, p. 51), similarly writes, "… because forms of action and interaction are always negotiated and confirmed as actors with different interests and interpretations (…), slippage between institutional templates and the actualities of daily life is probable. In such slippage resides the possibility of social innovation". Usage of the conception of improvisation to explain organisational change owes much to Weick (1993), who brings in the allegory of theatrical improvisation, where organisation design (pp. 348–351):

> …tends to be emergent and visible only after the fact. Thus, the design is a piece of history, not a piece of architecture…Design, viewed from the perspective of improvisation, is more emergent, more continuous, more filled with surprise, more difficult to

control, more tied to the content of action, and more affected by what people pay attention to than are the designs implied by architecture.

The conceptualisation of change as ongoing improvisation also reverberates with the emphasis on situated action, executed by practice researchers (Hutchins, 1991; Lave, 1988; Suchman, 1987). Hutchins (1991) contends that "several important aspects of a new organisation are achieved not by conscious reflection but by local adaptations" (p. 14). Rice and Rogers' (1980) concept of 'reinvention' and Ciborra and Lanzara's (1991) notion of 'designing-in-action', similarly ricochet the situational improvisation ideas narrated herein. In the context of a volatile and uncertain world, the managerial task is conceptualised as 'muddling through with a purpose' and achieving a succession of small or 'first order' changes (Levy, 1986). This kind of situational change process is well orchestrated by Escher's Metamorphose series, where, as the artist explains, through the changing times, "a dynamic character is obtained by a succession of figures in which changes of form appear gradually" (Escher, 1986, p. 120). Each variation of a given form comes about through a series of ongoing and situational improvisations, variations, and adjustments mediated through previous such variations, eventually leading to fundamental changes.

Some thinkers on change management take technology as the principal and relatively independent force for bringing about change. The ***technological imperative perspective*** accords little discretion to any organisational manoeuvring. Under this perspective, it is the adoption of new technology which creates anticipated changes in organisations' structures, processes, routines, circulation of information, and performance (Blau, Falbe, McKinley & Tracy, 1976; Carter, 1984; Cimini, Boffelli, Lagorio, Kalchschmidt, & Pinto, 2020; Leavitt & Whistler, 1958). Such organisational concepts of technological imperative echo a broader stream of technological determinism, which is so pronounced in a few studies in economic analyses (Heilbroner, 1967), socio-historical studies (Winner, 1986), contemporary culture (Smith & Marx, 1984) and social determinism constitute a continuum (de La Cruz Paragas & Lin, 2016). In the absence of any significant role for any organisational actor, such perspective nullifies any possibility of proactive or pre-emptive organisational change. Further, the deterministic logic of such managerial proponents of technological imperative is discordant with the fluid, open-ended and flexible nature of many of the new technologies, which are susceptible to significant user customisation (Malone, 1994).

Planned change models, in contrast, assume that managers as organisational actors are the primary architects of organisational change. These actors consciously and conscientiously initiate, execute and roll-out changes in anticipation of opportunities to increase or expand organisational performance. Such models have been predominant in organisational change literature, and are represented through various theoretical formulations such as force field analysis (Lewin, 1951), contingency frameworks (Burns & Stalker, 1961; Dunphy & Stace, 1988; Galbraith, 1973; Miles & Snow, 1984), innovation theories (Hage & Aiken, 1970; Meyer & Goes, 1988; Zaltman, Duncan, & Holbek, 1973), practitioner-oriented recommendations for organisational efficacy (Deming, 1986; Hammer & Champy, 1993; Peters & Waterman, 1982) and comparison of chaos, complexity, and contingency theories (Lartey, 2020).

Many a work on such planned organisational change espoused techniques for premeditated transition management (Beckhard & Harris, 1977; Benne, Chin, & Bennis, 1976) and many of the examples in those works were of changes at the unit level in an organisation (Mumford, 1972; Ottaway, 1976). However, many other theorists looked critically at the endeavours for large-scale organisational change and concluded that such attempts only had superficial effect, if at all. Large organisations, quite often, were perceived to be dominated by extremely pluralist and incremental methods of decision-making, consequent upon political restraints on perfect choice (Alford, 1975; Hickson, 1985; March & Simon, 1958).

Punctuated equilibrium models, which posit change to be fast, episodic, and far-reaching, have been espoused in contrast to the gradualist models, which postulate that organisational change is slow, incremental, and cumulative (Meyer, Goes, & Brooks, 1993). Gersick (1991, p. 12) writes, "relatively long periods of stability (equilibrium) [are] punctuated by compact periods of qualitative, metamorphic change (revolution)". Punctuated models have informed macro research of long-term changes in various industries (Abernathy & Clark, 1985; Romanelli & Tushman, 1994; Tushman & Romanelli, 1985). However, amplifications of this perspective have offered a mixture of the punctuated equilibrium and gradualist rationalities (Mintzberg, 1987). More recently, Uotila (2018) examines how environmental turbulence and complexity influence the temporal patterns of incremental and radical organisational change. Both the punctuated equilibrium perspective and its hybrids are based on the primacy of organisational stability. Whether refining a currently existing situation or moving on to a new one, the underlying postulation is that the favoured condition for the organisation is a steady state or "equilibrium" of sorts (Mintzberg, 1987).

In view of the limitations in punctuated equilibrium perspective, many organisational thinkers, such as Tichy (1983), Kimberly and Quinn (1984), Pettigrew (1985) and Pennings (1985) have probed the possibility of **radical transformation** and the conditions required to bring it about. Lundberg (1984), for example, writes of strategies for bringing in major organisational transitions. Researchers, such as Von Braun (1990), hypothesise that fundamental to success in a competitive environment is the ability to innovate and take radical steps which would position an organisation considerably ahead of competitors. Some researchers have probed for the characteristics which would distinguish transformational change (Child & Smith, 1987; Hinings & Greenwood, 1989; Van de Ven, Angle, & Poole, 1989).

Organisational ecology theorists (Aldrich & Mueller, 1982; Hannan & Carroll, 1992; Hannan & Freeman, 1989) consider the population of organisations as evolving. The evolution of organisational forms is recorded by the disparities in the comparative size of total populations of firms. The proponents of the *population ecologists' theory* "maintain that differential rates in the entry and exit of organisations cause populations to gradually evolve to fit the technical and economic constraint of environmental niches" (Meyer et al., 1993, p. 73) and this phenomenon in turn gives rise to the evolution and growth of organisations.

In the case of **institutional theory**, organisations per se "experience pressure to conform to the normative expectations of their institutional environments" (Meyer, et al., 1993, p. 73). Many authors consider institutional change a method in which institutions are subject to a choice process wherein concerned players compete to administer institutional changes useful to their direct interests (Mahoney & Thelen, 2010; Ostrom, 2005). Others conceptualize institutional change as an evolutionary process happening naturally through an uncoordinated process concerning many dissimilar players (Williamson, 2000). Some scholars seek to amalgamate these two approaches in what can be categorised as an equilibrium view of institutions (Greif, 2006; Kingston & Caballero, 2009). More recently Lander and Heugens (2017) explore the complementarities between ecological and institutional theories and argue that a rapprochement would be worthwhile.

The **innovation theory** emphasizes process and product innovations in business, management, and market development that lead to the evolution of organisations. Damanpour and Schneider (2008, p. 497) made a distinction between innovation and adoption of innovation.

They branded innovation as a process culminating in a result which is new to an organisational population. On the contrary, they identified adoption of innovation as a process, resulting in assimilation of a process, product or practice new to the adopting organisation.

organisational Metaphor Approach. Cameron and Green (2009), drawing upon the works of Morgan (1986), closely examine the inner mechanisms of organisations while analysing organisational change. For the purpose, they use four organisational metaphors and explain how organisational change works. These four metaphors proffer the most pertinent understanding into organisational change management (Cameron & Green, 2009; Morgan, 1986). These four metaphors are organisations as machines, political systems, organisms, and as flux and transformation.

According to Morgan (1986), "When we think of organisations as machines, we begin to see them as rational enterprises designed and structured to achieve predetermined ends". Cameron and Green (2009) further expound on this and include humdrum operations, articulated structures, clearly spelt-out job descriptions, explicitly laid-out procedures and standards and well-organised parts working in unison to form the whole of the organisation. Cameron and Green (2009), as a logical corollary, deduce: each employee should have a singular line manager; management should be through individual objectives; and command and control, along with rigorous enforcement of discipline, should be adhered to for ensuring performance. Just as a well-designed and well-oiled machine, rightly constructed and connected, moves in specific direction when force is applied appropriately, an organisation would also successfully move from State A to State B in clearly delineated stages, if everyone works as per plan. This is the ideal metaphor for a simple project management approach to change, where everything gets fitted into Gantt chart and everybody performs as a part of a machine.

Immanent in the metaphor of organisation as machine are a few significant beliefs on organisational change (Cameron & Green, 2009), viz., those in authoritative positions can change an organisation from the current state to an approved end state; resistance, which shall crop up inevitably, is required to be managed; and change can be effected, if it is well-planned and well-controlled.

Heavily drawing upon Morgan (1986), Cameron and Green (2009), aver that the metaphor of organisations as Political Systems, is beneficial for understanding the role of power and conflict within organisational life. Morgan (1986) notes:

Many people hold the belief that business and politics should be kept apart...But the person advocating the case of employee rights or industrial democracy is not introducing a political issue so much as arguing for a different approach to a situation that is already political.

There are some central beliefs of this metaphor (Cameron & Green, 2009): in Organisational life, no one can stay out of organisational politics; building support for one's approach within the organisation is essential, if one wants to achieve anything; one needs to understand the power dynamics within the organisation, as there are significant political maps which supersede the documented organisational structure; and coalitions between individuals are more important than actual work teams.

The metaphor of organisations as Political Systems suggests that everyone who occupies an organisational space is in the heart, not only of a human system, but also of a system which is governed by opposing forces and pulls on limited resources. Diverse players in the show have diverse degrees of power and the cognisance and management of these players effectively results in change initiatives. It is on the understanding of who is an enabler and who is a disabler, who gains and who loses, who supports and who opposes, and tailoring one's change strategy accordingly, that the success of a change initiative eventually rests. Immanent in this metaphor are a few postulates: change cannot be effected, unless it is it is supported by power and authority; the wider the support, the more successful the change initiative can be; and change measures should be supplemented by clear-cut understanding of the political map as to who the winners and losers of change may be.

The metaphor 'organisations as Organisms' compares organisations to living, adaptive systems. Morgan (1986) states, "The metaphor suggests that different environments favour different species of organisations based on different method of organizing ... congruence with the environment is the key to success". Thus, in a stable organisation with predictability, a rigid, bureaucratic structure would flourish, whereas in a less stable environment fraught with uncertainty, an unstructured organisation would quite likely evolve.

Cameron and Green (2009) relate the metaphor of 'organisations as Organisms' to an open system, where organisations are not distinct singular entities, but are composed of a conglomerate of internal, interrelated sub-systems functioning in an external milieu, affected by movements and interfaces all through. Further, the organisations are so designed as to balance the necessities of the environment with the niceties of individual and group needs.

The metaphor of 'organisations as Organisms' is based on the assumption that an organisation is able to adjust itself and endure in the eco-system (Cameron & Green, 2009), if it is well-made to meet the requirements of the environment and if the social needs of individuals and groups within the organisation are satisfied. The metaphor rests on the beliefs that the movement of information between different sub-systems and the environment is key to the organisation's success and it is of paramount importance to maximize the fit among individual, team and organisational needs for the organisation to sustain and succeed. This metaphor is also based on some beliefs about organisational change: changes are done only in response to variations in the external environment; individuals and groups are to be made aware of the need for change so that they can acclimatize and adapt; and involvement and psychological backing are essential strategies for organisational success.

The metaphor 'organisations as Flux and Transformation' views the organisation against the backdrop of uncertainty, complexity and chaos. Cameron and Green (2009) assert that this metaphor views organisations essentially as a constituent of the environment, rather than as entities distinct from it. This metaphor is consistent with a tempestuous and turbulent environment, where the managers are not in complete control of change. Morgan (1986) asserts, "In complex systems no one is ever in a position to control or design system operations in a comprehensive way. Form emerges. It cannot be imposed".

The fundamental postulates under the metaphor of 'Flux and Transformation' are: order naturally spring up out of anarchy; organisations undergo a natural self-renewal process; key tensions are vital in the emergence of novel ways of managerial procedures; and the formal organisational structure epitomizes only one of the many aspects of organisational life. Immanent in this metaphor are certain assumptions about organisational change: change, emerges, it cannot be managed; managers are a part of the systems they manage, or rather a part of the whole environment; tensions and conflicts are a significant aspect of emerging change; and managers act as enablers for ushering in change as they empower employees to exchange opinions and try and resolve substantial differences.

It has been observed that Morgan's metaphors simultaneously serve as "relatively static reflections", providing an historical exposition of organisational theory) and "relatively dynamic projections", inspiring the postulations of futuristic organisational images (Oswick & Grant, 2016).

Concluding Observations

In general, almost all schools of thought espouse that organisations have been undergoing changes owing to internal and external environmental factors that come in various forms, such as change in management, organisational development, and implementation of new initiatives as per the needs of time. In this context, a study of different models of change is necessary, which is taken care of in the succeeding chapter. However, there is no gainsaying that organisations in the process of change build newer structures and managerial edifice. The history of business shows that such changes quite often have a decisive influence on the performance of organisations (Chandler, 1992). A firm's growth or decay centres on whether organisational changes occur and the way they are managed. It may be proper to concede that without the vision, conceptualisations and initial actions, it would not be possible to establish and manage an organisation. It may also be prudent to maintain that as an inference of the dynamic focus on organisational modification, it is necessary to reflect on the entrepreneurial role within the organisation and its transformations (Penrose, 1959). However, it is equally important to see that the organisation and the market in which it functions co-evolve. Further, such co-evolution moves the borderline between the firm and the market (Langlois, 1992; Langlois & Robertson, 1995).

4 Models of Organisational Change

The speed of change has never been greater than in the present business environment (Balogun & Hope Hailey, 2004; Burnes, 2004; Carnall, 2003; Kotter, 1996; Luecke, 2003; Moran & Brightman, 2001; Okumus & Hemmington, 1998; Paton & McCalman, 2000; Senior, 2002). Not just in technology, but in business models and competitive dynamics as well, the speed of change is so fast that what an executive knows today, may become irrelevant by tomorrow (Neubauer, Tarling, & Wade, 2017).

Due to the importance of organisational change, its management is becoming a highly required managerial skill (Senior, 2002). Graetz (2000, p. 550) suggests "Against a backdrop of increasing globalisation, deregulation, the rapid pace of technological innovation, a growing knowledge workforce, and shifting social and demographic trends, few would dispute that the primary task for management today is the leadership of organisational change." Change management is defined as "the process of continually renewing an organisation's direction, structure, and capabilities to serve the ever-changing needs of external and internal customers" (Moran & Brightman, 2001, p. 111).

This Chapter investigates four famous models postulated by management analysts. These models – Kurt Lewin's Three Step Model, John Kotter's Eight Step Model, Nadler and Tushman's Congruence Model and Peter Senge's Systemic View – form the fundamental aspects of understanding the importance that change management has come to occupy in present day organisations.

Kurt Lewin's Three Step Model

Kurt Lewin, a social scientist and a physicist, is known as the 'father of change processes' (Pathak, 2011). He espouses a cornerstone model for understanding change processes, known as Unfreeze – Change – Refreeze Three-Step model of change. Lewin's theory is mainly based

DOI: 10.4324/9781003191346-4

on changing behaviour contingent upon psychological determination (Kritsonis, 2005; Pathak, 2011). He states that to bring change in the organisation, three phases of change can be followed, largely based on human behaviour (Odendaal, Robbins, & Roodt, 2004). These include:

a. Unfreezing the status quo;
b. Movement to a new state or Changing behaviour;
c. Refreezing the new change to make it permanent.

To start with the first phase, 'Unfreezing' can be defined as the "breaking away from the way things have been done" (Harper, 2011, p. 18). In this phase, Kurt Lewin investigates how change is considered to provide equilibrium after two opposite forces interact with each other. These opposite forces are the 'driving forces' and the 're-straining forces' (Harper, 2011; Kritsonis, 2005). The former aims to bring and promote change, while the latter seeks to manage the status quo of the organisation. The maintenance of the status quo helps achieve stability and equilibrium in the organisation. In case organi-sations wish to change internally and adapt to external change, they need to move from this equilibrium stage and over individual (or employee) resistance and group conformity. For the unfreezing system to become effective, the 'driving forces' must always supersede the restraining forces. This is when the 'unfreezing of the status quo' is required. As per Lewin's analysis, such unfreezing can be understood through his 'Force Field Model', where all surrounding elements like habits, customs, people, and attitude act as forces in bringing in change (Harper, 2011). Unfreezing can be achieved by pursuing three main elements. These include: increasing the driving forces that direct behaviour away from the status quo; decreasing the restraining forces that thwarts things move away from existing equilibrium; and lastly, finding a combination for the two elements listed herewith (Kritsonis, 2005). Lewin's model presupposes that change is a difficult process and the approach to be applied must be different in different situations:

> The 'unfreezing of the present level may involve quite different problems in different cases. Allport...has described the 'catharsis' which seems necessary before prejudice can be removed. To break open the shell of complacency and self-righteousness it is sometimes necessary to bring about an emotional stir up. (Lewin, 1947, p. 229)

Building on Lewin's ideas, Schein (1996, p. 27) comments that the key to unfreezing '...was to recognise that change, whether at the individual or group level, was a profound psychological dynamic process'. Schein (1996) emphasises three processes required for unfreezing: disconfirmation of the validity of the status quo; the induction of guilt or survival anxiety; and creating psychological safety. He argues that: '...unless sufficient psychological safety is created, the disconfirming information will be denied or in other ways defended against, no survival anxiety will be felt and consequently, no change will take place' (Schein, 1996, p. 61). This implies that those affected need to feel safe from any sense of deprivation and then only they can embrace the changes.

As Schein (1996, p. 62) notes, the goal is not reached by unfreezing per se; it "...creates motivation to learn but does not necessarily control or predict the direction". The second phase or the 'movement to new change' can be defined as "identifying and trying new ways to do things or new things to do" (Harper, 2011, p. 18). In the second phase of 'changing behaviour', organisation considers the changing behaviour to be the step towards achieving a new level of equilibrium. Three ways this change can be achieved are: persuading employees to change their ways and adapt to change; persuading employees to work towards new quests and relevant information; and finding ways to connect groups of employees with great leaders (Kritsonis, 2005).

The third phase 'refreezing' can be defined as "reinforcing the new ways or new things to do" (Harper, 2011, p. 18). The third phase of refreezing takes place after the changes take place. In most cases, changes are considered short-lived, and employees have the tendency to revert to their old behaviour. To avoid such complications, steps need to be taken, which Lewin refers to as 'refreezing' the change policies (Harper, 2011). To implement this, the organisation should try to find new equilibrium where there is a balance between the 'driving' and 'restraining forces' in the changed scenario. Lewin suggests that new formal and informal mechanisms in terms of policies and procedures can be implemented to maintain the changes adopted (Kritsonis, 2005). New behaviour should be harmonious with the balance of the setting of the learner or it could result in a new scenario of disconfirmation (Schein, 1996). This is the reason Lewin's model takes effective change as a group activity. Unless group norms and procedures are altered, changes to individual behaviour will not be sustained. In the organisational setting, refreezing requires changes to organisational culture, norms, policies and practices (Cummings & Huse, 1989).

Sarayreh, Khudair, and Barakat (2013) criticize Lewin's three-phase model as too simplistic and deficient in living up to modern complex needs. Even as Lewin's model has become outmoded in the last two decades (Dawson, 1994; Hatch, 1997; Kanter, Stein, & Jick, 1992), its impact continues to be indelible. So much so that Hendry (1996, p. 624) comments: scratch any account of creating and managing change and the idea that change is a three-stage process which necessarily begins with a process of unfreezing will not be far below the surface.

Many organisations recognize the value of this model, and the model has been used by large companies to reorganise their marketing functions. The reason for effectiveness in applicability of Lewin's model is that, the model not only offers suggestions on how changes can be brought about, but also depicts how changes adopted can be maintained and continued to be pursued for further organisational development. Lewin's was one of the first theories to recognize that change is a constant which is relational and happens through interaction. In today's world of uncertainty, Lewin's theory provides a premise to perceive and cope with uncertainty as a source of change, which, at the crux of it, is what Lewin meant by the process of 'unfreezing' (Van Nistelrooij, 2018).

John Kotter's Eight Step Model

Over the past decades, companies have been trying to build their organisations by reinventing organisational structures. The underlying fundamental facet of this reinvention is to change the way business is conducted. One of the most popular models for planning, implementing, and sustaining this change is the 'Eight-Step Change Model' introduced by John Kotter (Kotter, 1995). The model investigates the change in organisations in eight steps.

i. **'Establishing a sense of urgency'** refers to the need to examine market and competitive realities (Kotter, 1995) on an emergent basis. This helps in identifying and discussing crises and solving them to create greater opportunities. Bold actions, characteristic to a strong leadership, are normally vital for creating a strong sense of urgency (p. 43). Kotter (1995) further espouses that leaders must communicate this information "broadly and dramatically". Kotter (1996, p. 44) recommends the use of consultants as a tactic for crafting a sense of urgency and challenge the status quo. Armenakis, Harris, and Mossholder (1993) strengthen Kotter's statement by suggesting the recruitment of sources outside the organisation. An analytical report compiled by a consulting agency can be used as an instrument to add believability to the need for change. A study by Gist, Schwoerer, and Rosen

(1989) supports the contention that a message generated by more than one source, particularly if external to the organisation, is given a greater air of credibility and confirmation.

ii. **'Create a guiding coalition'** refers to the formation of groups to make the employees learn how to work in team (Kotter, 1995). This guiding coalition should be made up of people with the following characteristics (Kotter, 1996, p. 53):

    a. **Position power:** enough key players so others cannot block progress;

    b. **Expertise:** all relevant points of view should be embodied so that informed decisions can be taken;

    c. **Credibility:** the group should be seen and respected by those in the firm, so the group's decrees will be viewed seriously by others; and

    d. **Leadership:** the group should have enough proven leaders, so it can drive the change

        Lines (2007) observed that change agents with substantial position power are more successful at implementing change than change agents with low amounts of position power but high expertise, even as both are positively correlated to the success of implementation of organisational change. In a review of organisational change in three specific case studies (viz. Cool aid case, Municipality of Saanich, First nations Mountain Pine Beetle initiative), Cunningham and Kempling (2009) established the importance of a guiding coalition in assisting the change process.

iii. **'Develop a vision and strategy'** for the specific change simply refers to the creation of vision and goals that need to be achieved by the company (Kotter, 1995). The importance of a well-defined vision for the change process is well-researched in change literature. In a case study on the human resource systems at the US Environmental Protection Agency, it has been observed that a shared vision of the project's outcome is essential (Wright & Thompsen, 1997). Whelan-Berry and Somerville (2010) agree that change vision is a key part of change process.

iv. **'Communicating the vision and strategy'** is a critical element of the organisational change process as it can diminish uncertainty (Bordia, Hunt, Paulsen, Tourish, & DiFonzo, 2004), decrease ambiguity and can affect organisational change (Nelissen & van Selm, 2008). Uncertainty is defined by Salem and Williams (1984) as inability to describe, predict, or explain. 'Communicate the vision and strategy for the specific' refers to the finding of tool to communicate the new vision and strategies (Kotter 1995).

v. **'Empower the employees for action'** refers to the encouragement given to employees to make them take risk and make innovative development (Kotter, 1995). A study of empowerment of frontline employees in 16 luxury hotels in seven European countries establishes that multiple aspects, such as structure, attitudes of supervisor, and training, play important parts in employee empowerment (Klidas, Van Den Berg, & Wilderom, 2007).

vi. **'Generate short-term wins'** refers to planning improvements, achieving the improvements, and recognising those who work for the improvement (Kotter, 1995) in the short term. Willie Pietersen, former President of Lever Brothers' Foods Division in the USA, states that all-encompassing change can be a long-drawn out process; hence it is imperative to generate wins (Pietersen, 2002) in relatively shorter time frames. A few quick wins, albeit small, can create confidence and instil the self-assurance that bigger wins are thinkable. This would build up the momentum towards the longer-term goals (Pietersen, 2002). Celebrating opportunities and rewarding small successes also provide employees and management the comfort that their endeavours are heading in the right direction (Marks, 2007; Reichers, Wanous, & Austin, 1997).

vii. **'Consolidate gains and produce core change'** refers to all aspects that can bring changes and development in areas like organisational vision, structure, policies, system, etc. that are not in sync with the envisaged changes (Kotter, 1995). Pfeifer, Schmitt, and Voigt (2005) contend that validating the reliability of vision and strategy through the usage of results already achieved is the main goal for rallying the initial successes. Management requires such first successes to consolidate further change process, and partially validate the short-term costs defrayed through the change initiatives (Pfeifer et al., 2005).

viii. **'Anchor the new change in the culture'** refers to institutionalising new approaches in terms of articulating new behaviours and corporate success, as well as ensuring leadership development and succession (Kotter, 1995). Jacobs (2002) emphasizes institutionalisation of such changes that have comparative endurance and staying power over a period or that "has become part of the ongoing, everyday activities of the organisation".

These eight approaches of Kotter are known for giving straightforward guidance for organisational planning to bring changes (Petersen et al., 2014; Sabri et al., 2006). In fact, Kotter's studies are addressed more to end users or managers involved in managing the change, rather than to any scholarly audience. Managers are more prone to look at literature, having a practical point of view, rather than at scholarly empirical literature. The model has been scrutinised in various practitioner-oriented contexts by various researchers (Hackman, 2017; Kang et al., 2020; Kuo & Chen, 2019; Lambert, 2019). Even as amalgamation of all eight steps in a methodical manner is an important component of Kotter's model, this aspect of maintaining the order has not been investigated much in a heuristic manner.

Nadler and Tushman's Congruence Model

The Nadler-Tushman Congruence Model was formulated in 1977 by David A. Nadler, Michael L. Tushman and Nina G. Hatvany. This model shows how all the components and variables of organisational structure are related to each other in bringing about change in the organisation (Nadler, Tushman, & Hatvany, 1980). This model offers an opportunity to examine the transformation process in such a way as would stimulate thoughts on what is required to be executed against the backdrop of an organisational milieu.

The structural components of the organisation consist of task, individuals, and formal and informal elements that shape the organisation (Nadler et al., 1980). *Task* refers to the inherent work which is supposed to be carried out by the organisation; *individuals* refer to the employees of the organisation, and identification of the roles played by these employees in building the organisation; *formal organisational elements* refer to all the processes, procedures, methods and structures of the organisation that help the employees to perform the tasks in the organisation; and *informal organisation* refers to the unstated values and procedures that influence the organisation, where individuals are conditioned to work with them, besides the formal elements that constitute the organisation (Nadler et al., 1980; Palmer, 2005).

According to this model, since organisation is an open system, all these components are interdependent on one another. The point of interdependence is understood through the interaction of the organisational structure consisting of three processes, known as the input, throughput or the transformational process, and output (Nadler et al., 1980). Organisation allows these processes to get influenced by the environment and the concomitant variables therein, facilitating its change during the transformational process. The organisations which can maintain these variables in a stable condition during transformational processes, or in other words, the organisations which are able to keep these components "fit", experience development and growth (Nadler et al., 1980). When the components are disrupted during the process, organisations suffer dysfunctions, making the performance level go down, and subsequently leading to the downfall of the organisation (Nadler et al., 1980). The interactions of these three processes are explained herein:

a. ***Input.*** Inputs are the factors, which are considered 'given' and which remain relatively stable in enabling the organisation to function. There are four inputs, which explain the behaviour of people in the organisation, and act as the factors that stop the employees from taking drastic steps. These inputs include: **Environment; Resources; History; and Strategies.** *Environment* refers to all the larger forces that surround and envelope the organisations as external influences. These forces include the "markets, suppliers, governmental and [other] regulatory bodies, labor unions, competitors, financial institutions, special interest groups, and so on" (Nadler et al., 1980, p. 38). Environmental factors are the most influential factors in initiating and managing change. These factors are vital in conditioning the organisational functioning and longevity (Nadler et al., 1980). There are three main functions of environment that determine organisational analysis. Firstly, environmental forces put market pressures on the organisation, propelling it improve production in terms of quality and quantity and maintain its competitive position in the business world (Nadler et al., 1980). Secondly, the environment may limit the production and working of the organisation by posing threats and regulations, such as by governmental bodies (Nadler et al., 1980) or may even put technological constraint (Palmer, 2005) in case of some organisations. Thirdly, the environment can also provide new opportunities to the organisation at the same time (Nadler et al., 1980). *Resources* consist of all the tangible and intangible assets that are internal to the organisations. These include human resources, technological and financial capital, information, raw materials, brand and premium value of the organisation in the market, etc. (Basu & Palazzo, 2008; Nadler et al. 1980). Resources help organisation determine the extent to which it would move towards new ventures. *History* refers to the past of the organisation that impacts its functioning. Learning from the past mistakes, crisis or strength helps the organisation to take firm and correct decisions in building the organisation. In many successful organisations, important key strategic decisions such as appointing a leader, recruitment of employees, decision making, etc. are determined by reflecting on the history of the organisation (Nadler et al., 1980; Palmer, 2005). Perhaps *strategy is* the most important input in the organisation. It refers to the entire set of fundamental decisions taken by the organisation against the backdrop of environment, resources and history (Nadler et al., 1980). Strategy making, and strategy management take all other inputs into consideration while formulating plan and policies for organisational growth and development (Palmer, 2005; Nadler et al., 1980). Strategic decisions normally revolve around issues such as prospective markets to explore, product and services to scout for in such markets, strategies the organisation may pursue to compete with rival business groups, policies and procedures required to be formulated, ways and means to make decision making efficacious and the like (Nadler et al., 1980). Thus, postulating strategy is not only about policy making, but also about processing the policies and getting positive results out of the policies. Proper application of all the inputs by human resource and leaders results in adaptation to change that brings in growth and development of the organisations.

b. ***Throughputs.*** The major components of the transformational process that remain interactive while transforming the inputs into outputs include the human capital, the task and jobs of the people and organisation, the managerial structure of the organisation and the employees, groups, units, and sub systems of the organisation (Nadler et al., 1980).

c. ***Output.*** Output refers to 'what the organisation produces, how it performs, and how effective it is', after putting the inputs into application (Nadler et al., 1980). While analysing organisational output, certain factors that can be marked off to understand organisational performance and effectiveness include: evaluation as to whether the organisation has achieved its goal; how effective its achievement of the strategic goal has been; how much has the organisation been engaged in using the resources of the organisation in pursuit of these goals; whether it has increased or depleted resources; and whether the organisation shows adaptability to everyday changing society (Nadler et al., 1980). Output is a product of contributions from various individuals, departments and units of the organisations. Garnering effective output guarantees the longevity of the organisation, while ineffective results compromise the organisational working and functionality (Nadler et al., 1980).

Nadler-Tushman's congruence model, unlike the models discussed earlier, emphasizes the relationship between the external environment and the internal structure of the organisation. The external fit enhances the functioning of the internal structure. The greater the congruence between the two, the more effective an organisation can grow, change, and adapt to the market economy. The model emphasises the interaction between each of the constituents rather than the constituents themselves. The model draws attention to all the dimensions of organisational life. Successful change is pivoted on understanding and making suitable changes in all the sub-systems. Even as the model emphasizes internal stability over a period and homogeneity across like systems, some form of learning is implicit in the model for the purpose of adaptation (Teece, 2018).

Peter Senge's Systemic Model

Learning and change are inextricably connected. Peter Senge, the organisational learning guru, in his two books *The Fifth Discipline* and *The Dance of Change* discusses the role of learning in successful transformational change.

In "The Fifth Discipline", Senge talks about 'learning organisations', which he defines as, "…organisations where people continually expand their capacity to create the results they truly desire, where new and expansive patterns of thinking are nurtured, where collective aspiration is set free, and where people are continually learning how to learn together" (Senge, 1990, p. 3). Successful change management platforms are created on the principles of organisational learning and necessitated through the continual flux of volatile environments. Indeed,

> Our environments are more and more complex, more and more interdependent, more and more fleeting, more and more unstable, and more and more unforeseeable. In addition, this shift of change of growing complexity is continually accelerating. Thus, this new context continually requires greater capabilities of adaptation, relegating to us the responsibility of our learning, and it is asking for the creation of a culture of continuous change and learning. (Lapointe, 1998, p. 2, as cited in Fillion, Koffi, & Ekionea, 2015)

Senge identifies five essential components of a learning organisation:

i. **Systems Thinking** – the way we look at and resolve problems and construe solutions;

ii. **Personal Mastery** – defining what we want to achieve and how we achieve the same;
iii. **Mental Models** – deeply held philosophies about how the world works;
iv. **Shared Vision** – shared values, beliefs and objectives in the organisation;
v.   **Team Learning** –sharing experience and expertise and learning as a group.

Based on interaction with the change leaders of various organisations, on their experiences of successes and failures, Senge built a framework that holds the dynamics of the change journey in his book 'The Dance of Change'. A basic premise of this book is that organisations grow out of the ways their employees think and act. Organisational learning is a result of individuals participating in new conducts of thinking and acting and relating together which in turn leads to an augmentation of the organisational ability for change. Senge et al. (1999, p. 10) argue that,

> Sustaining any profound change process requires a fundamental shift in thinking. We need to understand the nature of growth processes and how to catalyse them. But we also need to understand the forces and challenges that impede progress, and to develop workable strategies for dealing with these challenges. We need to appreciate 'the dance of change', the inevitable interplay between growth processes and limiting processes.

Senge and colleagues argue to 'focus on understanding the limiting processes' (1999, p. 8) which are identified as four:

i.   Reaching the 'difficult' problems, having first addressed the 'easy' ones, summed up in the phrase: 'We've picked all the low hanging fruit';
ii. Reaching the limit of management commitment, when engulfed by change;
iii. Reaching the risky 'un-discussable' which may lead to discords; and
iv. Lack of systemic thinking, tackling symptoms rather than pro blems.

Senge et al. (1999) and Senge and Kaeufer (2000) ascertain the challenges of sustaining change. The three main challenges concern fear and anxiety, a concern with performance measurement and the dangers of innovations becoming isolated from the rest of the organisation. Sustainability is regarded as a stage in the long-term process which begins with implementation and diffusion, then follows with continuous improvement.

To bring sustainable change, Senge argue that managers should start with bringing small changes, instead of trying to bring in whole new changes, and the small changes would grow slowly and systematically in regular pattern (Joseph & Reigeluth, 2010). In the end, these small change initiatives bring in radical changes. Such initial small changes should be steered through a group of informed stakeholders who make up a pilot team. Senge believes that the effectiveness of the pilot team as a change agent is more as the individuals involved cultivate a personal stake. Once an effective team is formed, it needs to deal with what Senge calls the ten challenges centred around three phases in the life cycle of change.

Phase I: Initiating Change

 i. 'We don't have time for this stuff!'
 ii. The pilot team should be spared to spend as much time as they need on the change programme, even if it implies reducing other work commitments.
 iii. 'We have no help!'
 iv. If the team requires training and help from anyone in the organisation, it should be allowed.
 v. This stuff isn't relevant'
 vi. Some members of the team should be able to communicate the significance of the change programme to the organisation.
 vii. 'They're not walking the talk!'

It is of very important that the members of the pilot team and change leaders symbolise the values that they are championing.

Second Phase: Sustaining Momentum

 i. 'This stuff is…'
 ii. Personal anxieties and suspicion towards the change is required to be addressed through transparent and candid communication.
 iii. 'This stuff isn't working!'
 iv. The pilot team needs to be aware that the programme might not be initially successful; yet, it is imperative to stick even in the face of preliminary challenges.
 v. 'They're acting like a cult!'

The pilot team should be reachable to the rest of the organisation and the actions they espouse should be open and transparent.

Third Phase: Redesigning the Organisation

i. 'They never let us do this stuff'.
ii. The pilot team should have the authority to act and take things to logical conclusion.
iii. 'We keep reinventing the wheel'.
iv. The group should take cognisance of previous successes and build on the same.
v. 'Where are we going?'

The pilot group must have a focus and an achievable vision.

Senge felt that by practising these guiding principles, it would be feasible to create a learning organisation, amenable to change.

Concluding Observations

A tabular presentation of Comparison of Change Models is given in the Appendix. Comparison is done on three counts: Kezar's approach (2011) of classifying change based on degree of change, scale of change, focus of change and intentionality of change; Beer and Norhia's (2000) hard and soft approaches; and Cameron and Green's (2009) metaphorical approach of classifying change as if occurring in machines, political systems or organisms, or just as cogs in the giant wheel of a juggernaut continually revolving under winds of flux or transformation.

The primary reason for the emergence and evolution of a plethora of change models has been the characteristic of the business environment itself, which has been in a continual state of volatility. Further, the universal models of change management are insufficient to describe the diversity of approaches used by organisations. Most organisations, in fact, have made rapid transformative change using a directive leadership style (Dunphy & Stace, 1993). In view of this, organisations are taking situation-specific, multi-dimensional approaches to change management, rather than adopting any universal model. Accordingly, the book elaborates change, resistance, organisational strategy, business environment, factors determining change and work practices from multiple dimensions.

5 Resistance to Change

Quite often change initiatives are confronted with different degrees of resistance (Oreg, 2006). Employees' resistance to change is largely a psychological phenomenon and it greatly affects the success of change management initiatives in organisations (Choi & Ruona, 2011). Folger and Skarlicki (1999) aver that "organisational change can generate scepticism and resistance in employees, making it sometimes difficult or impossible to implement organisational improvements" (p. 25). Maximisation of the perceived benefits of organisational change initiatives to a large extent depends on how effectually such initiatives "create and maintain a climate that minimizes resistant behaviour and encourages acceptance and support" (Coetsee, 1999, p. 205). Hence, it is quite necessary that organisations need to understand what essentially constitutes resistance (Giangreco & Peccei, 2005).

Theories on Resistance to Change

Organisational change is quite often an offshoot of personal change (Band, 1995; Choi, 2011; Dunphy & Dick, 1989; Steinburg, 1992). In order that organisational change becomes a success, it is essential that individual change comes about (Evans, 1994). Pursuant to the implementation of an organisational change initiative, individuals undergo a reaction process (Kyle, 1993). Scott and Jaffe (1988) characterise this process as consisting of four sequential phases: denial; resistance; exploration; and commitment. Inasmuch as change involves moving from a known realm to an unknown, it naturally and normally meets with resistance (Coghlan, 1993; Myers & Robbins, 1991; Nadler, 1981; Shimoni, 2017; Steinburg, 1992; Zaltman & Duncan, 1977). Since experiencing change is an individualised process, it varies from individual to individual (Carnall, 1986). Further, different individuals have different abilities and volition to adapt to change (Darling, 1993).

DOI: 10.4324/9781003191346-5

Piderit (2000) observes that the conceptualisation of the term resistance encompasses three broad strands, viz. "...as a cognitive state, as an emotional state, and as a behavior" (p. 784). Armenakis et al. (1993) describe resistance as a cognitive state which they characterise as a "state of (un)-readiness" (2000, p. 785). Such 'states of (un)-readiness' are offshoots of individuals' having instinctive negative thoughts largely comprised of faulty or irrational thinking (Beck, 1988; Burns, 1990). Further, such instinctive internal negative thought processes emanate from misapprehensions and defective assumptions, resulting in emotional and behavioural turbulence (Corey, 1996). Coghlan and Rashford (1990) argue that workplaces are replete with such maladaptive thought processes. These are cognitive distortions and figments of imagination rather than reality, are internalised without any valid testing, and are just assumed to be the truth (Coghlan, 1993). Such dysfunctional cognitive processes need to be corrected in time; otherwise, resistance to change will magnify (Coghlan, 1993; Miller & Yeager, 1993).

Failure to adapt emotionally to change propels resistance (Spiker, 1994). Organisational changes lead to feelings of fear, denial, anger, loss, sadness and frustration (Spiker & Lesser, 1995). Losses or changes in roles or responsibilities can lead to expressing emotions of fury, despondency or low self-esteem (Sullivan & Guntzelman, 1991). According to Dent and Goldberg (1999), individuals, during a change process, may not be resisting change actually; rather, they may be resisting the loss of status or comfort. As they proclaim, "it is time that we dispense with the phrase resistance to change and find a more useful and appropriate model for describing what the phrase has come to mean – employees are not wholeheartedly embracing a change that management wants to implement" (p. 26). Often, resistance to change is a defence mechanism triggered by frustration and apprehension (Piderit, 2000).

Depicting resistance in terms of behaviour is common in change literature. For instance, Brower and Abolafia (1995) describe resistance as a specific kind of action or inaction, and Ashforth and Mael (1998) outline resistance as deliberate acts of commission, such as insubordination, or omission. Shapiro, Lewicki, and Devine (1995) propose that inclination to deceive authorities implies resistance to change. Sagie, Elizur, and Greenbaum (1985) express compliant behaviour to be indication of diminished resistance. "Managers have many terms to describe resistance: pushback, not buying in, criticism, foot-dragging, and so on. And they may perceive as resistance a broad spectrum of behaviors they don't like-from an innocent question to a roll of the eyes or overt sabotage" (Ford & Ford, 2009). Even though technological innovation is willingly accepted in everyday life, at the workplace such changes lead to resistance and find diverse manifestations such as active/passive, or open/clandestine (Župerkienė, Paulikas, & Abele, 2019).

Psychological and Behavioural Dimensions

It is generally observed that individuals make assumptions about change processes, appraise them and give meaning to them. They develop feelings about them, and then react to them, rather than mechanically resisting future changes (Hendrickson & Gray, 2012; p. 52). In the process, individuals define "cognitive and behavioral efforts to manage (reduce, minimize, or tolerate) the internal and external demands of the person-environment transaction that is appraised as taxing or exceeding the person's resources" (Folkman, Lazarus, Gruen, & DeLongis, 1986, p. 572). This process is otherwise christened as coping strategies. The psychological factors that mediate such cognitive processes have been researched by psychologists over time.

Personality dimensions are considered having important mediating effects on change readiness, resistance and coping behaviour in the context of change management. Responses to organisational change are influenced by several personality traits, viz. locus of control, change-related self-efficacy, self-esteem, positive affectivity, openness to experience, tolerance for ambiguity, and risk aversion.

Rotter (1966) espouses the concept of locus of control as one's perception of one's ability to exercise control over the environment. It has been observed that employees with internal loci of control have more positive attitudes towards experiencing changes than employees with external loci of control (Lau & Woodman, 1995; Nelson, Cooper, & Jackson, 1995).

Change-related self-efficacy is one's perceived ability to handle change in a given situation and deliver on one's objectives, despite the rigours of the change (Wanberg & Banas, 2000). Low efficacy levels have been correlated with withdrawal from the demands of the job (McDonald & Siegall, 1992), coupled with "defensive behaviors", such as resistance to change and turf protection (Ashforth & Lee, 1990).

Self-esteem refers to positive self-evaluation and it has two dimensions, viz. 'competence' and 'worth' (Gecas, 1982). Competence denotes individuals feeling efficacious, and worth refers to how the individuals value themselves. Individuals with greater self-esteem appear to have more "cognitive resources", which permit them to tide over adverse conditions (Baumgardner, Kaufman, & Levy, 1989; Liu, Zhang, Chang, & Wang, 2017; Spencer, Josephs, & Steele, 1993; Steele, 1988).

Positive Affectivity (PA) is reflected in personality characteristics such as well-being, self-confidence, liveliness, sociability, and affiliation. Watson and Clark (1997) have noted that the PA concomitantly echoes individual differences in boldness and adventurousness, and hence "high scorers desire change and variety in their lives and become bored or dissatisfied when (change) is absent" and tend to "seek out intense, stimulating environments" (p. 776). Thus, high-PA managers generally cope with changes with ease, as they derive a sense of satisfaction from it.

Openness to experience of change is associated with intelligence, insight, originality, imagination, tolerance, and curiosity (Goldberg, 1992). McCrae and Costa (1986) found that openness was positively related to the use of effective coping strategies in dealing with stressful life events. Whitbourne (1986) noted that openness to experience was positively associated with identity flexibility in work as well as family roles. It is generally perceived that employees open to experience are less likely to perceive change as worrisome, and cope more efficiently with organisational change.

Stanley Budner (1962) define tolerance for ambiguity as "the tendency to perceive ambiguous situations as desirable", whereas the intolerance of ambiguity as "the tendency to perceive (i.e., interpret) ambiguous situations as sources of threat" (p. 29). Rush, Schoel, and Barnard (1995) observe that items assessing tolerance for ambiguity are correlated with several aspects of coping with change among employees.

Lopes (1994) has theorised that risk aversion is a function of differential attention to various stimuli in risky situations. Many studies considering risk aversion as an individual difference have found that individuals who are loath to risk view novel and risk-oriented situations negatively and seek to withdraw from such situations (Cable & Judge, 1994; Gomez-Mejia & Balkin, 1989), thus demonstrating low coping behaviour.

The psychological dimensions resulting in changes in the cognitive processes get manifest in divergent behavioural indicators. Giangreco (2002) takes up 12 items for tapping 12 different actions regarding individuals' response to change. The 12 items are synthesised into two factors depicting pro-change and anti-change behaviour. The individuals' responses, clustered on these two factors, result in a matrix of behaviour categorised into four possible categories.

Except for the individuals who are in the fourth category, i.e., those who are confused about the change, all the other categories exhibit three distinctive behavioural response patterns. The detailed behaviour patterns are depicted herewith:

i.   **High Pro-Change and Low Anti-Change:** The first category encompasses individuals who frequently engage in pro-change behaviours, and never indulge in anti-change behaviour. This implies that they facilitate change and endeavour to actualise it.

ii. **Low Pro-Change and Low Anti-Change:** The second category includes individuals who exhibit a low occurrence of both pro-change and anti-change behaviours. They do not assist the change by engaging in any helpful behaviours. They do not also show any behaviour which would construe disagreement with change.

iii. **Low Pro-Change and High Anti-Change:** The third category includes individuals who report never engaging in pro-change behaviours, but frequently demonstrating anti-change behaviours. They do not approve the change and either personally exhibit anti-change behaviours or ratify someone else's activities against the change.

iv. **High Pro-Change and High Anti-Change:** The fourth category encompasses individuals who exhibit a high incidence of both pro-change and anti-change behaviours. It is supposed that these pro and anti-change behaviours are interspersed over time, since nobody can possibly engage in contradictory behaviours at the same time.

Causes of Resistance

Some theorists and analysts have come up with their own theory on what causes the 'resistance to change'. Kanter (1985) postulates many reasons for resistance to change such as: fear of the unknown; loss of control, face, and competency; lack of support and confidence; the need for security when change happens; poor timing in terms of adapting to change; force of habit to stick to the old form; and harbouring resentment towards change among employees, leaders, and organisation as a whole (Kanter, 1985). O'Connor (1993) theorises that there are several causes for resistance that provoke the employees and the organisations. These causes include:

a.   Lack of belief among the employees that there is a need for change;

b.   Employees, leaders, and management groups have different attitude, needs, and description of change;

c.   Many organisations also do not have consensus among the employees and leaders to come up with goals for change;

d. Many of them also do not believe that change can be adapted and accommodated easily;
e. organisations also fail to exhibit confidence for change (O'Connor, 1993).

Waddell and Sohal (1998) give a broad view of the causes of resistance to change. They identify rational factors of individual employees as the prime cause for which individuals find difficulty in welcoming change. They also identify non-rational factors like adapting to new office space, etc. among difficulties in adapting to change.

Kasemsap (2015) came up with internal and external factors regarding resistance to change. Internal factors are mostly related to the 'lack of response to creativity' among employees (Kasemsap, 2015). The reasons for such lack in creativity include:

a. fast and complex change environment that does not allow proper situation analysis;
b. possessing reactive mind-set that does not allow people to pursue change, since they think that change brings inevitable obstacles;
c. inability of leaders, employees, and the organisation to come up with clear strategic vision and commitment (Kasemsap, 2015).

External factors regarding resistance relate to cultural and political deadlocks to adapt to change (Kasemsap, 2015). In such cases, there are difficulties in implementing cultural and value changes against traditional structures. Accordingly, leaders fail to act since they become reluctant and afraid of the uncertainty that changes will bring.

Concluding Observations

Some more insight is given by Kyle (1993) on what causes resistance to change. He asserts that individual employees are the most difficult to change, and since change needs to start from individual employees, resistance occurs. Organisational change requires employees and their job behaviour to change. Every organisation has its own culture, which sets the rubrics for employee job behaviour. Organisational culture affects employee motivation, facilitates employee and organisational learning, modulates communication, and helps inculcate organisational core values, group dynamics and conflict-management, and thus becomes a huge factor impacting organisational change.

6 Organisational Culture and Organisational Change

Organisational culture is defined as:

> A pattern of basic assumptions – invented, discovered, or developed by a group as it learns to cope with its problems of external adaptation and internal integration – that has worked well enough to be considered valid and, to be taught to new members as the correct way to perceive, think and feel in relation to those processes. (Schein, 1985, p. 9)

Pareek and Rao (1999, p. 24) defined organisational culture as:

> Cumulative, crystallized and quasi stable shared lifestyle of people as reflected in the presence of some states of life over others, in the response predispositions towards several significant issues and phenomena (attitudes), in the organized ways of filling time in relation to certain affairs (rituals), and in the ways of promoting desired and preventing undesirable behavior (sanctions).

The essentials of the outline of culture that emerges is a set of learned and common responses to the organisational environment, tasks and problems (Schein, 1984; Turner, 1971). This process of learning is what is required to be facilitated by the organisation by producing a mindset amongst individual members which are prompted by organisational membership (Baum, 1987; Crozier, 1964; Hummel, 1982; Jackall, 1988; Merton, 1940; Mierke & Williamson, 2017; Whyte, 1956). Through this process organisational culture in turn improves organisational effectiveness (Deal & Kennedy, 1982; Denison, 1990; Kilmann, Saxton, & Serpa, 1985; Peters & Waterman, 1982; Varghese, Das, & Jebamalai, 2016).

DOI: 10.4324/9781003191346-6

Organisational Culture and Cultural Adaptation

Employees' job behaviour within the organisation broadly depends on the 'cultural adaptation' of the individual employees to their job and working environment, 'political connection' or the relationship that employees need to forge with other employees, leaders, and even stakeholders, and aligning expectations of the employees and organisations into unison (Watkins, 2003). Such process of cultural adaptation is to begin from the time of the induction (or on-boarding) of new recruits down to their working days. Many organisations have the tendency not to expose their culture for fear of scaring away the new recruits; instead, this should be avoided by giving a briefing on the company's history, culture and goals to make employees or workers effective in their jobs (Watkins, 2003; Watkins, 2019).

It is generally believed that management can create a consistent organisational culture around its core values. The process would normally begin with the crafting of a vision statement, a corporate philosophy or mission, articulation of a corporate strategy and crafting of a set of core values. The strategy would not be confined to economic goals, but would also include statements about what kind of organisation the company will be – its character, the values it espouses, its relationships to customers, employees, communities, and shareholders (Ocasio & Joseph, 2018; Sinclair, 1993). Murphy (1989, p. 81) has observed "that ethical business practices stem from an ethical corporate culture".

Some criticise this approach and methodology of creating a Unitarian culture. Nicholson (1984, p. 264) has argued: "the practice of management is itself a component of culture...Management cannot control culture for attempts to control cultural variables themselves constitute part of the culture". Many believe that strong organisational cultures do possibly support conformism and eliminate opposition and do thereby generate "strategic myopia" and rigidity (Bourgeois, 1984; Lorsch, 1985). In the arena of business ethics, where issues are continually in the flux, such narrowness can be a disastrous flaw (Drake & Drake, 1988). Research on cultural adaption, according to Sinclair (1993), raises questions as to "whether culture is propaganda, and training is indoctrination" (Pascale, 1985; Schein, 1967).

In response to such critique, an alternative approach to creation of culture has been to understand the 'value differences of subcultures and the terrain of controversy within the organisation' (Gregory, 1983; Sinclair, 1993). There has been increasing attention of researchers on the 'degrees of variance in values and ideologies between hierarchical and functional levels of the organisation' (Arogyaswamy & Byles, 1987) and the necessity "to understand the paradoxes and complexities of our belief system" (Ackroyd & Crowdy, 1990, p. 12). Reed and Anthony (1992) observe that for cultural management to be successful, rather than cosmetic or deceptive, it will have to comprehend comparative values and belief systems. Quite a few researchers believe that values and norms that are of permanent and paramount influence on behaviour subsist within the discordance of subcultures, rather than permeate through a pervasive organisational corporate culture (Latta, 2020; Martin & Siehl, 1983; Wilkins & Ouchi, 1983).

Cross-Cultural Dimensions

Many cultural theorists have delved into the nuances of cross-cultural differences among nations and regions. Hofstede Cultural Dimension Model helps understand the cultural differences or diversity between nations from different dimensions, based on empirical researches and depicts the cultural mapping technique employed in management studies. Hofstede's work was a result of the findings of an employee attitude survey of 100,000+ employees undertaken across IBM's global operations between 1967 and 1973 across 40 countries. He identified five variables as determinants of organisation's culture, while analysing that an organisation is driven by temporary practices and values (Yolles, 2006). The five dimensions are: 'Power Distance', or the degree to which power is equally and legitimately distributed as perceived by the members; 'Uncertainty Avoidance', or the extent of maintaining conformity for avoidance of ambiguity; 'Masculinity/ Feminity', or the organisational preference for accomplishment and heroism over weak qualities; 'Individualism/Collectivism', or the survival of individuals within the social group, as against dependent membership; and 'Long/Short term Orientation', or espousal of short or long term values (Yolles, 2006).

This model has captured the greatest attention when it comes to studying change management through cross-cultural dimensions needed in the business management world (Baumüller, 2007). The fact that globalisation has necessitated the leader or managers to garner connection across countries through technological usage, accords a high external validity value to this model (Baumüller, 2007).

Trompenaars and Hampden-Turner, building on the Hofstede Model, enunciated the 'Seven Dimensions of Culture' model, in which they assert that employee job behaviour is culturally determined, and so, the successful implementation of practices is reliant on wider understanding of cultural differences (Ahlstrom & Bruton, 2009; Beugré, 2007; Trompenaars & Hampden-Turner, 2004). The complications that arise for managers when cultural borders are crossed concern mainly the diminishing effectiveness of their proven management processes. In cross-cultural scenarios, managers must understand cultural differences and recognise that there is no "one best way of managing" organisations, largely because of the pervasiveness of such cultural differences (Trompenaars & Hampden-Turner, 2004; Trompenaars & Woolliams, 2003). Trompenaars' belief was that effective employee job management can be enhanced through understanding cultural differences, and that these cultural differences can be used for gaining competitive advantage by building cultural synergy across the organisation.

As part of adapting to change in organisation, employees should also have 'political connection', facilitated by the organisation so the employees improve their working behaviour. The organisation should engage in helping new employees in forging relationships and identifying stakeholders (Watkins, 2003). This will allow employees to identify the tools of the organisational network and possibly identify alliances in bringing development to the organisation. Employees should also 'align expectations' with that of the organisation (Watkins, 2003; Watkins, 2019). Most of the time, both the employees and organisations do not possess a clear and distinct view of one another; instead, they put on their best positive faces as to what can be expected from each other. In this scenario, there should be an effective connection or aligning of their expectations, which can lead to improvement in employees' job behaviour.

Concluding Observations

The success of an organisation depends on how well the individual interests of employees are aligned with the organisational goals and objectives. Such organisational alignment is not an accident. It requires leaders to combine divergent individual interests and variegated viewpoints, synthesize them from the organisational point of view and align expectations of the employees and organisations.

7 Leadership and Organisational Change

Earlier in Chapter 3 it was examined how organisational change works in actuality in the context of organisational metaphors such as machines, political systems, organisms, and as flux and transformation. Here, an exposition is made as to how the leadership role varies vis-à-vis each organisational metaphor. Further, the leadership style of change leaders has a significant role in the change implementation process. This chapter deals with roles of leaders vis-à-vis divergent leadership styles.

Roles of Leaders vis-à-vis Change Metaphors

Using the machine metaphor paradigm demands a strict project management approach, marked by a leadership style characteristic of an architect or a grand designer. The style is manifest with heightened emphasis on expertise in and efficacy of project planning process and rigorous execution thereof. The metaphor symbolises an action plan that involves definite drawing out of the strategy to move from stage A to stage B and involves watchful planning, managing, monitoring and controlling of the process.

This metaphor involves change through taking care of interests. This necessitates a superior focus on handling stakeholders and a heightened emphasis on ensuring that key players as well as opinion makers are aligned with the change strategy. It also requires ensuring that possible winners are inspired enough, and possible losers' requirements are taken care of. In this paradigm, the leaders need to have perceived power and they need to delegate such power to the change agents.

The organism metaphor requires that the leader be proactive and vigilant on a continuous basis. The leaders under this paradigm are required to identify and engage change agents, who would screen the

DOI: 10.4324/9781003191346-7

environment unceasingly. The leaders need to foster an enabling organisation, so change agents can learn to take cues from the environment and discharge proactive actionables for bringing in changes that are required.

The 'flux and transformation' metaphor involves change through emergence. Under this paradigm, it is championed that change per se cannot be overtly managed; rather, it emerges. The leaders' role involves identification of the areas of tensions and conflicts within the organisation and on the boundary lines and engage change agents to monitor and manage such areas. Under this paradigm, the role of the leader is to enable and facilitate the emergence of change, rather than direct and monitor it.

Leadership Styles and Organisational Change

Kurt Lewin categorised three major leadership styles – autocratic, participative and delegative (Lewin, Lippitt, & White, 1939). In the autocratic style, the leader takes his own decisions without any consultation with the employees. In the participative style, the employees are involved in the decision-making process and in delegative style, the employees are permitted to take decisions, even as the leader is responsible for the results.

Likert identifies four leadership styles – exploitative authoritative, benevolent authoritative, consultative and participative (Likert, 1967). Leaders with exploitive authoritative style instill fear among employees and generally they have no concern for others. Benevolent authoritative style users do impart rewards contingent on performance, but they take all major decisions without any involvement of other employees. In the consultative style, decisions are still taken by the leaders, but the leaders listen to the ideas of followers. In the participative style, decisions are taken jointly with the followers.

Burns and Bass use the terms transformational and transactional leadership style (Bass, 1985; Burns, 1978). Transformational leadership style is characterised by four factors: idealised influence or charisma; inspirational motivation; intellectual stimulation; and individual consideration (Bass, 1985). Transformational leaders act as role models, generate a sense of identification with a shared vision, inculcate a sense of pride and faith in followers, motivate and empower followers, inspire followers to rethink their conventional wisdom and give individual attention and recognize individual needs (Bass, 1999). Transformational leadership activates higher-order needs and induces transcendence of self-interest for the sake of the organisation (Bass, 1985; Yukl, 1989). Transactional leadership style is characterised by two factors: contingent reward; and management by exception (Bass, 1985). The management by exception factor has been divided into two elements: active; and passive (Lowe, Kroeck, & Sivasubramaniam, 1996). Transactional leaders operate through clarity, contingent reward, attempting to meet material and psychological needs in exchange of desired services or behaviours through communication (Jacobsen & Salomonsen, 2020; Syndell, 2008). In contrast with transformational leadership, transactional leadership focuses on the satisfaction of lower-order individual needs and is exemplified by task-oriented behaviours (Bass, 1990).

Sometimes a situational view of leadership style is taken and is christened as change-oriented leadership, which is also considered to have key elements which are typical of transformational leadership, "albeit at a lower level of abstraction, at a greater level of situational specificity" (Herold, Fedor, Caldwell, & Liu, 2008). It can be understood as more of an application of behaviours within the situational context of change implementation. In fact, as is stated by Chawla, Sujatha, and Shukla (2016), successful leaders remain flexible to adopt best possible style and approach required for different leadership scenarios.

Researchers have attempted to study the connection of leadership styles in facilitating change through their linkage to Resistance to Change (RTC) and commitment. RTC and commitment are sometimes perceived as disparate management issues, or unrelated phenomena in organisational development (Coetsee, 1999). However, a study by Judson (1991) links commitment to resistance and shows that they are opposites of a single spectrum. Judson's model lists gradual phases ranging from active resistance at one end, to indifference in the middle, and to acceptance at the other end. In so far as RTC and commitment lie in one continuum, the change practitioner must target both commitment and resistance simultaneously (Johnson, 1991).

Transformational leadership influences followers by empowering them to join in the process of organisational transformation. Transformational leaders can influence major changes in the attitudes and assumptions of different stakeholders towards change, building commitment towards the organisation's mission, objectives and strategies (Yukl, 1989), by augmenting employees' work engagement and perceptions of attractive change consequences (Faupel & Süß, 2019).

Concluding Observations

When it comes to driving organisational change, leaders play a critical role in setting the tone for what is acceptable within a company. They design and implement different strategies to bring in the requisite culture for organisational change and transformation. Leaders crystallise the vision for change so that others can seek to actualise it. They set the mission of an organisation and empower employees to achieve that mission. The choices they make have a ripple effect on all the systems and processes in the organisation. More so, on the Human Resource Management processes, such as employee recruitment, engagement, employee performance, and rewards and recognition systems, which eventually brings in the requisite organisational change.

8 Human Resources and Organisational Change

Shukla and Rizvi (2009), while examining HR's role in change management, especially in the context of mergers and acquisitions, hold the primal significance of HR's role, starting from the stage of due diligence. It is observed that less than one third of mergers and acquisitions produce value and the primary reason is lack of focus on people issues and leadership. This is true in every other change management context. Ihlenburg (2019) posits that in most of cases, suboptimal results in change management are due to mistakes in execution at the level of human resources and recommends practical wisdom as an effective means of bringing fruition to change management initiatives.

Change Management Plan

To have successful fruition of Change management programmes, HR needs to assess the readiness of the organisation and employees for change. This involves consideration of the scheduling of the change agendas, the speed required for its execution, its length in time, and the employees' knowledge, skills, and abilities (KSA) to execute the impending change. These factors are considered the 'hard issues' of change management which, if overlooked, can lead to the untimely cessation of change programmes (Sirkin, Keenan, & Jackson, 2005).

Looking at the requirement of speed for bringing in change, HR must have a plan for change in place. If change agenda is required to be executed with speed, HR needs to reduce the number of people to be involved in the process, as increased number would reduce the speed of execution. In such a scenario, HR may need to sensitise leadership to be wary of resistance. If a limited number of employees is involved for efficacy, there is a possibility that employees may feel unheeded; they may contest the change process. Conversely, when speed is not a predominant

DOI: 10.4324/9781003191346-8

consideration, the organisation can think of broad-based employee participation, to facilitate ownership (Kotter & Schlesinger, 1979).

Actualisation of the Change Vision

HR, working in combination with leadership, must ensure a detailed and vibrant imagery of what the changed scenario would look like, so it supplements the change vision and propels the employees to strive to bring it to the present (Cummings & Worley, 2009). HR should ensure managerial commitment to the change at all levels and incessantly throughout the change process. At the slightest display of managerial insincerity to the change process, the large mass of population would like to slip back to the pre-implementation phase, making change unlikely to happen (Sirkin et al., 2005).

HR should paint in lucid details the hiatus between the current scenario and the changed one, depicting clearly the need for change and the opportunities the business could garner, if the desired modifications take place. Thus, HR should create a situation of what is called 'physiological disconfirmation' and bring the employees to the brink from where they can clearly perceive the necessity and beneficence of change (Cummings & Worley, 2009). This can also be perceived as a scenario of 'reframing of business' (Essentials, 2006). By reframing, the workforce can take a step back, appreciate the necessity and/or advantage of the change, shift gears on the mental plane and rally behind the change.

Communication Matrix

HR should have a comprehensive communication plan in place. To be precise, there should be a matrix of communication, which should embody timelines, dates, data, targets, possible questions and doubts emanating from incipient resistance, along with their detailed answers involving adequate facts, figures and analytics. When sufficient details are not shared with employees or a veil of secrecy shrouds the actual truth about change, the grapevine, rumourmongering and storytelling emerge to fill in the gaps and negativism runs rife to thwart the process of change (Patterson, 2002). Through a comprehensive communication plan, management can speak with confidence while communicating about the status and desired change (Clampitt & Berk, 1996) and take into account the expectations and the requirements of all the participants in the change process (Bucăloiu & Tănăsescu, 2019).

It is a well-researched finding, held true across several management communication methods (Furst & Cable, 2008), that employees unconsciously use their feelings of trust or mistrust towards a messenger to accept or reject a message being communicated. Messengers who elicit allegiance, support, belief and fondness from employees can more successfully communicate messages of change as compared to those who do not. In view of the paramount importance of communication in change management programmes, HR should devise and administer a messenger identification strategy across all levels of the organisation which should focus on spotting leaders who are liked and trusted and hence can act as change messengers (Fox & Amichai-Hamburger, 2001).

The communication strategy needs to be tolerant to dissent. Dissensions need to be encouraged to be voiced. HR would ensure employees' buy-in by taking note of such ideas and anxieties. This would ensure creation of a sense of procedural justice leading to greater change acceptance (Fox & Amichai-Hamburger, 2001). Further, this could also show the mirror to the management and allow them to do mid-way course corrections in the eventuality of insurmountable obstacles. Many great companies have introduced innovative communication strategies which help in introspection and course corrections. Intuit India, which is a financial software company, in the business of development and marketing of financial, accounting, and tax preparation software and related services, in an endeavour to 'listen' truly to its employees, has promoted the practice called 'Screw-ups of the Month'. It gives a common forum to employees to get together and discuss issues and understand what went wrong and why, and how to salvage and ameliorate the situation (Intuit, Great Place to Work, 2019).

Rewards and Recognition Strategy

HR must have a rewards and recognition strategy in place to recognise and felicitate the early, though small milestones of change, so that it gets institutionalised. Celebrations of small achievements ushers in a feeling that change is possible. The best time to identify such small wins is early and often (Amabile & Kramer, 2011). Small accomplishments would have domino effect, build great momentum and spiral into eventual transformation.

The change agents' role should be specifically recognised, and HR must ensure the sustainability of change by building adequate support systems for the change agents. Being the people who push the change forward and see it happen, the role of the change agents is of prime importance in the entire process (Balogun & Hope Hailey, 2004). The change agents should not be allowed to burn out, lest the entire programme should lose momentum and slip into the older ways. Quite often, change agents would need some space for themselves and some psychological distancing from the rest of the employees. It is essential that change agents have their own office space where they can give vent to their feelings and be open among themselves and with management without criticism or retribution (Cummings & Worley, 2009).

One of the definite ways to recognise the initiators of change is to implement change ideas in a reasonably short time frame. Zee Entertainment Enterprises Ltd. (ZEEL), a worldwide media brand offering entertainment having presence in over 173 countries and catering to over 1.3 billion people across the globe, has institutionalised a system 'Change you want in 30 Days'. The initiative encourages people to express openly their concerns at the workplace. Propped up by a strong execution and implementation team carrying out the approved changes proposed by employees, the initiative was instrumental in bringing out several changes in the organisation (Zee, Great Place to Work, 2019).

Resistance Management

As the backbone in managing the organisation, there are many tools through which resistance can be managed and changes can be brought inside the organisation by the Human Resource Team or the Human Resource Development (HRD) (Simms, 2005). Following are some of the tools given by theorists Kotter and Schlesinger (1979), which brings out a general understanding of how HR can make individuals and organisations overcome resistance to change.

a. **Education and Communication:** Education has become the most important tool in lessening resistance to change among employees. HR needs to communicate ideas of change to the employees so that the latter understand what changes can bring about, and how changes can be dealt with and adapted to (Kotter & Schlesinger, 1979).

b. **Facilitation and Support:** In most cases, change usually requires upgrades in skills among employees. For example, when employees transition from individual contributors to managers' roles. In such cases, the HR needs to come up with proper training and practice to be imparted to the employees to adapt to change (Kotter & Schlesinger, 1979). In 2016, 100% of the new managers at Adobe underwent an internal programme, 'New Manager Orientation', geared at providing the right information, education and skills to help the new managers to be successful at Adobe (Adobe, Great Place to Work, 2019).

c. **Negotiation and Agreement:** Education and training alone cannot solve the issue in adapting to change. In fact, to overcome resistance to change, both the employees and the organisation need to effect changes. The employees can become more flexible in their roles in the work situation, while the organisation can rearrange working hours and change payment, incentive, etc., as may be expedient (Kotter & Schlesinger, 1979).

d. **Co-option:** Everyone has his/her set of skills, and it differs from one employee to another. To overcome resistance to change, individuals should be fitted according to their skills. This will bring faster and better changes (Kotter & Schlesinger, 1979).

Concluding Observations

It goes without saying that insofar as organisational change occurs for, with and through people, the Department responsible for people processes has an important role to play in times of change. Organisations quite often plan their development process from their current state to future desired states. It not only involves planning for growth, production, productivity, expansion and profitability, but also for augmentation of organisation-wide effectiveness through better systems, processes and instrumentalities to support such change. There are several high performance work practices (HPWP) which have been devised by Human Resources to support such change management, which deserve to be examined in detail.

9 High Performance Work Practices (HPWPs) to Support Change Management

High performance work practices (HPWPs) have become the subject of wide range of studies and have also gained prominence in the literature on the working of organisations (Tamkin, 2004). However, HPWP has been neither consistently defined nor identified (Baker, 1999; Becker & Gerhart, 1996; Delaney & Goddard, 2001; Murphy, Torres, Ingram, & Hutchinson, 2018; Wood, 1999). HPWPs have been differentially named as high-performance work systems, alternate work practices and "flexible work practices" (Delaney & Goddard, 2001).

In practices studied by academicians, analysts and organisations, elements such as skills, participation, empowerment, communication and compensation have become the driving force of HPWPs. For analysts such as Kirkman, Lowe, and Yaung (1999), there are five characteristics which guarantee high performance: self-managing work teams; employee involvement, participation, and empowerment; total quality management; integrated production technologies; and learning organisation. HPWPs are most effective when they are implemented in combination, as an overlapping set of measures (Pfeffer & Veiga, 1999).

HPWPs necessitate huge investment in employees for augmenting employee skills, knowledge, motivation and flexibility for facilitating their ability and the opportunity to offer positive contribution into workplace decisions and enactments (Van Buren & Werner, 1996). Companies in turn expect such empowerment for enabling employees to adjust swiftly to changing product and labour market surroundings, and to improve operational efficiency and organisational performance (Becker & Huselid, 1998; Cappelli & Neumark, 2001). Numerous studies, sometimes considering both the costs and the benefit aspects of HPWPs (Huselid, 1995; MacDuffie, 1995), do find a strong link between them and organisational performance.

Orlitzky and Frenkel (2005) observe that a wide gamut of the HPWP programmes, including divergent model specifications with

DOI: 10.4324/9781003191346-9

their underpinning assumptions, appeals to many, despite variable empirical evidence that shows the need for theoretical and procedural refinement (Becker & Gerhart, 1996; Becker & Huselid, 1998; Dyer & Reeves, 1995; Garg, 2019; Gerhart, Wright, McMahan, & Snell, 2000; Guest, Michie, Conway & Sheehan, 2003; Guest & Peccei, 2001). Research shows substantial differences in performance of employees which can be attributable to HRM practices, which in turn reinforces that implementing excellent HR practices is of paramount significance, because of its contribution to success in the aftermath of powerful forces of change unleashed from the Fourth Industrial Revolution, viz. volatility, uncertainty, complexity and ambiguity in the business environment (Turner, 2020). Guest (1997) suggests that there is a growing body of evidence corroborating a relationship between HPWP and organisational performance, but not much on why such association exists. The mechanism of the link between HPWP and organisational performance is considered a 'black box' with empirical and theoretical gaps (Luthans & Sommer, 2005).

Companies need to innovate constantly if they are to stay ahead of competition. Further, for the purpose of making alterations to organisational strategy and processes for remaining competitive, companies need to innovate. High-performance work practices result in organisational change and promote organisational creativity (Jeong & Shin, 2019). Nicholson, Rees, and Brooks-Rooney (1990) contend that HR has an important role to play in enabling the process of innovation. HPWPs help employees to think for themselves and to manage their own work (Lawler III, 1986; Pfeffer, 1994) and thus facilitate innovation. HPWPs promote innovation through managerial decentralisation allowing discovery and usage of knowledge, encouraging multi-disciplinary team practices and promoting knowledge acquisition and putting such knowledge to good use (Laursen, 2002). Burns and Stalker (1961) argue that the more organic the organisational culture is, the more it arouses innovation. Laursen (2002) supports that HPWPs create organic organisations by continuously moving decision-making downward. A few of the HPWPs are analysed here.

Performance Management and Feedback Mechanisms

In the present highly competitive environment, organisations must ensure peak performance of their employees continuously to compete and survive at the marketplace effectively (Prasad, 2006). The singular HR system that plays the most pivotal role is Performance Management, insofar as it enables organisations to clarify their vision and strategy and brings in strategy-consistent endeavours and behaviour. Thus, Performance Management System as a HPWP, is a great instrument to bring about planned change in organisations.

A performance measurement system enables informed decisions to be made and actions to be taken because it quantifies the efficiency and effectiveness of past actions through appropriate data. On the other hand, Performance Management has often been described as managing the Performance of an organisation or individual, in a futuristic manner.

In view of the persistent changes that business strategy goes through because of the continuous fluidity of the business world, performance measurement systems need to be vibrant, based on realities, and measure the cardinal issues impacting the business (Lynch & Cross, 1991). Colville and Millner (2011) state that "a trap that organisations can fall into is not recognising that the implementation of performance management is a change process."

Colville and Millner (2011) argue that in order for a Performance Management System to deliver an 'organisation strategy and vision', HR needs to have an awareness of the 'current state' and the 'desired state' of the organisation and its processes. HR should create a situation of what is called 'physiological disconfirmation' and bring the employees to the brink from where they can clearly perceive the necessity and beneficence of change (Cummings & Worley, 2009).

Performance appraisal of employees implies the assessment of their performance undertaken during a specific period of time. According to Beach (1980), "Performance appraisal is a systematic evaluation of the individual with regard to his or her performance on the job and his potential for development." The Performance appraisal process helps organisations to evaluate individually the employee's "behaviour and accomplishments over a specific period of time" (DeVries, Morrison, Shullman, & Gerlach, 1981).

Historically, performance reporting systems used to mirror facts about previous performance and were grossly inept at providing information about future performance. Performance measurement is the process of quantifying the efficiency and effectiveness of past action (Neely, Gregory, & Platts, 1995). A performance measurement system enables informed decisions to be made and actions to be taken because it quantifies the efficiency and effectiveness of past actions through appropriate data. This is one of the oldest and most universal practices of management (Tripathi, 2006).

The intense competitiveness of the economy and volatility of the economic environment forced many organisations to shift from reactive performance appraisals to proactive performance management in order to augment productivity and improve organisational performance. This was based on a realisation that it is more imperative to focus on outlining, planning and managing performance than simply appraising performance (Pareek & Rao, 1999).

In their book 'Managing Performance', Armstrong and Baron (2005) note the shift in terminology from performance appraisal to performance management, which they believe indicates a wider shift in the philosophy and content of the process: "Performance appraisal has a reputation as a punitive, top-down control device, an unloved system. Performance Management is a holistic, total approach to engaging everyone in the organisation in a continuous process, to improve everyone and their performance, and thereby the performance of the whole organisation. "Performance Management, is, in fact, a systematic process for improving organisational performance by developing the performance of individuals and teams (Armstrong, 2006).

Traditional accounting-based performance measures were characterised as being financially based, internally focused, backward looking and more concerned with local departmental performance than with the overall health or performance of the business (Johnson & Kaplan, 1987; Keegan, Eiler, & Jones, 1989; Neely et al., 1995; Olve, Roy, & Wetter, 1999; Skoog, 2020). Consequently, in the late 1980s and early 1990s there was a great interest in the development of more balanced performance measurement systems with the creation of frameworks such as supportive performance measures matrix (Keegan et al., 1989), the Strategic Measurement Analysis and Reporting Technique (SMART) pyramid, the Results/Determinants Matrix (Fitzgerald & Moon, 1996; Fitzgerald, Johnston, Brignall, Silvestro, & Voss, 1991) and the Balanced Scorecard (BSC) (Kaplan & Norton, 1992)

The Balanced Scorecard initially was designed as a performance measurement tool (Kaplan & Norton, 1992). As time passed, however, it emerged as a tool for implementing strategies (Kaplan & Norton, 1996) and a charter for defining the configuration of human, information and organisational capital with strategy (Kaplan & Norton, 2004). Thus, the essence of the Balanced Scorecard is cascading down of the organisational strategy into actionable result-oriented areas and its evaluation in a multi-dimensional paradigm. This involves not only financial parameters, but customer, internal processes and strategic capability perspectives as well.

The balanced scorecard concept has attracted a lot of research attention among academics and practitioners. According to Wiersma (2009), balanced scorecard, along with Activity Based Costing, is the most profound innovation in management accounting. In most of the developed world there are reports of major corporations experimenting with it (Speckbacher, Bischof, & Pfeiffer, 2003). Balanced Scorecard has received world-wide attention (Nørreklit, Kure, & Trenca, 2018) and has been endorsed by major Corporations around the world with the software market being inundated with a plethora of BSC application software (Wiersma, 2009).

Over the years, the inadequacies of the Key Result Areas and Competency Based Performance Systems have come out glaringly, no matter how balanced these may have become. These performance-management systems are criticised as having lost the utility of time in today's world. This is primarily because they are entrenched in prototypes for concentrating on and incessantly augmenting distinct jobs. These are offshoots or remnants of the paradigm of scientific management dating back to late 19th and early 20th century.

Frederick W. Taylor was the proponent of scientific management, which has since become the most widely-used principle for organising manufacturing and production. The basic tenets of scientific management are reduced to three rules – reducing complex tasks into simple ones, measuring each component of such job or task and rewarding proportionate to performance. Taylorism may have changed in form in the digital age but has remained the same in principle. Similarly, what is measured may have changed from the stopwatch-based time and motion to more complex Key Performance Indicators (KPIs) which could in turn get connected to the all-encompassing company goals. However, what is measured and weighted, has become ever more micro. In fact, technology itself allows time-and-motion studies to be taken to newer heights. The Human Dynamics Groups at MIT has devised a wearable device called sociometric badge, or sociometer, which measures the amount of face-to-face interaction, tone of voice, gestures, conversational time, physical proximity to other people, physical activity levels and the like. Such badges are being used in real time in organisations to measure individual and collective patterns of behaviour and predict the same. Motorola makes terminals that tie to warehouse workers' arms as much to assist in their efficacy as to monitor their activities. Several construction companies are these days using drones to monitor the progress of activities. The more the technology of measurement has advanced, the more power Frederick Taylor's successors have gained.

However, digital Taylorism is as disliked as its precursor. Measuring each small nuance of a job makes it bereft of its inherent beauty. Micromanaging for measuring of knowledge jobs confines a knowledge worker's capability to use his proficiency imaginatively.

Campbell (1990) conceptualises job performance as including "dimensions on execution of substantive tasks as well as elements focusing on motivational and interpersonal features." Subsequent literature on performance generally rivets on two aspects of job performance – task performance and contextual performance. Task performance basically involves completion of jobs and responsibilities embodied in the Job Descriptions and Key Result Areas (KRA), whereas contextual performance refers to activities that are not assigned or identified as a Key Result Area. KRA must make employees, functions or organisations more effective and efficacious, which includes attributes like liaising and collaborating and assisting others. It should also include *extra-role* activities performed of one's own volition, striving relentlessly with passion and persistence to complete tasks efficaciously, shielding the organisation's vision and objects, and tenaciously adhering to organisation's guidelines and values.

In the systems of micromanagement, manifest in digital Taylorism, there is no room for assessment of such contextual performance as voluntarily taking up group tasks or accomplishing tasks and assignments outside the KRAs.

The eras when employees were considered as a factor of production have advanced to a time when employees are acquired and engaged to help them realise their full potential for progression and performance. There has to be more emphasis on assessment of contextual performance (viz. task/Job not covered in KRA, voluntarily taking up assignment, defending organisational goals & values) rather than task performance, in today's world of remote connectedness and team or Project-based working. The process of PMS needs to help shape goals that are more volatile and unsettled, rather than a set of annualised Key Performance Indicators (KPIs). It needs to facilitate a process of obtaining and disseminating continual feedback rather than one at the end of annual or bi-annual appraisal cycle, because such feedbacks provided through the PMS mechanism once or twice in a performance cycle quite often are carried out more in the nature of routine activities, to be checked in the box.

Because of these reasons, many Companies, both in the international arena as well as in India have been doing away with such Performance Management Systems, of late. Companies such as GE, Microsoft, Gap, and Adobe Systems have disbanded their annual appraisal systems and are instead resorting to new initiatives to get continual feedback and provide meaningful training. These Companies have dropped ratings, rankings, and annual reviews. These companies want to provide objectives that are more volatile and unsettled than annual goals, recurrent feedback discussions rather than annual or semi-annual ones, progressive coaching for development rather than backward-focused rating and ranking and a greater emphasis on teams than on individuals.

The 21st century has ushered in an era of 'any time, any place' access to information, flexible work time, information on the go. Today people from around 20 countries can be part of the same Project and work for the same goal by forming a virtual team and unwind at the end of the Project. Such remote connectedness is fueled by technology. Contextual performance behaviours have become even more important in such work situations. Job descriptions give way to going the extra mile through remote connectedness and teamwork. Voluntarism and loyal steadfastness encapsulated in contextual performance become significant drivers for organisational performance and emerge as the most cardinal of behavioural competencies,

Contextual performance is differentiated from task performance in many ways.

i. First, task-related behaviours contribute directly or indirectly to the production of goods or delivery of services of the organisation (Borman & Motowidlo, 1993). On the contrary, contextual performance impacts the social and psychological environment of the organisation.

ii. A second way to distinguish is to consider behaviours that are set and agreed versus those that are not set, agreed or documented. Contextual performance behaviours are discretionary behaviours that are not prescribed. (Borman & Motowidlo, 1993; Motowidlo & Van Scotter, 1994).

iii. Thirdly, job-specific behaviours are offshoots of knowledge, skills and abilities (KSAs) and the KSAs differ depending on the job itself. Contextual behaviours, on the other hand, are more dependent upon other attributes resulting from personality factors (Hjalmarsson & Dåderman, 2020). Such attributes leading to contextual behaviour permeate through several of actions thereby forming a common discernable strand across many jobs.

Contextual performance can augment productivity through multiple means (Podsakoff, Ahearne, & MacKenzie, 1997). A few examples are given herewith.

i. Interpersonal co-operation, such as guiding colleagues on useful skills, or proffering alternative propositions, can enhance team efficiency in the immediate situation and over time, as "best practices" are shared throughout work groups and departments.

ii. Interpersonal enablement, involving supportive and considerate dealing of co-workers can aid in a manager's productivity by reducing time or energy spent on group preservation activities.

iii. Employee obedience to organisational processes allows managers to focus on higher-order organisational tasks other than mundane disciplinary or monitoring activities.

iv. Suggesting on plugging organisational imperfections and redundancies and ways to improve may give managers valuable pointers on how to improve productivity.

v. Employees demonstrating high levels of practicality or conscientiousness may voluntarily endeavour to grab new opportunities for acquiring new knowledge or developing new skills or abilities. This surely would facilitate the employee development process and would offload some pressure of employee development from the managers.

vi. Contextual performance also augurs well for customer satisfaction (Morrison, 1996). Careful employees go well beyond customer outlooks and are in the habit of bringing in what is called 'customer delight'.

Building Competencies and Training and Development

Performance is usually described as desired results, behaviours, attitudes, or mannerisms. Some argue that performance refers to the final consequence. Others argue that performance has to do with the behaviours people show while producing results. Human performance is a complex phenomenon incorporating process as well as outcome aspects (Kozlowski, Gully, Nason, & Smith, 1999). The process-oriented approach to performance focuses on the competencies as the knowledge, attitudes, and behaviour that yield performance outcomes. Heneman and Thomas (1997) indicate that as performance measures outcomes, it may measure results relative to the organisation's goals, while competencies represent how these results are attained.

An important component of Performance Management Systems has been competencies. The integration of competencies into performance management helps companies to identify and reinforce behaviours that lead to superlative performance. With a competency-based performance management system, the organisation delineates the performance criteria for each level so that employees know what competencies they must possess and master in order to grow. Companies can manage their talent pool more easily, perform succession planning, and build bench strength. In addition, it creates a basis for rewards and recognition and merit increases, and promotions.

Draganidis and Mentzas (2006) delineate the main reasons competency-based HRM is implemented by companies:

i. it provides identification of skills, knowledge, attitudes and capabilities required for actualisation of the organisational strategies and objectives;
ii. it emphasises on reducing competency gaps among employees in a project, job role or enterprise.

Competency gap analysis can identify the needed competencies, which can be linked with the equivalent learning objects (Draganidis & Mentzas, 2006). Greengard (2001) offers a discussion on the competency-based practice done by organisations; for example, Ford financial uses a skill and competency-based learning program that affords employee an opportunity to view information such as the skills and competencies needed for positions.

As one of the most quoted and referenced analysts on training and development of employees in management studies, Bauer (2010) has brought out research that covers all the dimensions of techniques in building competencies and training and development that modern organisations comprehend. She has developed a model consisting of four core factors known as the four Cs, which have been widely applied by many modern organisations. These four Cs are **Compliance, Clarification, Culture, and Connection** that employers or organisations need to help the employees to cultivate during their training and job performing process, in order to achieve organisational success (Bauer, 2010). **Compliance** deals with providing information to the new employees about the basic rules and regulations of the organisation. **Clarification** ascertains and ensures that the employees understand their work-related issues and find the onboarding process effective. **Culture** inculcates the organisational culture among the employees. **Connection** refers to the relationship and networks that the employees must establish within the organisation.

For reaping the right results of Training and Development interventions, today's organisations engage in the use of appropriate technology for training and development process, where e-learning is used as a platform to engage in multiple audience training programmes across various locations in the world (Pande & Basak, 2012). The availability of intranet allows all the information of the organisation to be compiled there. Further, handbook or information about the organisation is available as intranet link for employees to explore. In today's world, social media also provides an umbrella for networking among the employees, and the new generation web technologies allow cultural participation of the employees. It has become the conversational tool between the managers and employees, where words, pictures, videos and audio contents are easily transmitted among the group (Meier & Melar, 2014).

HR Competency Model for Change Management

The purpose of an HR competency model for change management is to use it for conducting HR Audit (Ulrich, 1997) and predicting how a person will perform the job; and evaluating whether a person fits the job profile (Ulrich & Brockbank, 2005; Spencer & Spencer, 1993). HR Change Management Competencies are defined as the right set of "knowledge (of change processes), skills (as change agents) and abilities (to deliver change)" (Ulrich, 1997, p. 68) as well as personality traits that can determine and predict the success of the individual job performance (Becker, Huselid, & Ulrich, 2001; Spencer & Spencer, 1993; Ulrich, Brockbank, Yeung, & Lake, 1995; Ulrich, Kryscynski, Ulrich, & Brockbank, 2017).

Uzunova (2012) has developed a framework outlining four competency realms composed of ten competencies for studying change management competencies. The four competency realms are: Transition Reinforcement Skills; Transition Enabling skills; Leadership skills; and Proactiveness. The first two realms, Transition Reinforcement Skills and Transition Enabling skills, are envisioned to reflect the process and the people aspect of the change. On the other hand, the latter two, viz. Proactiveness and Influential Skills, reflect the personal traits contributing to the increased HR effectiveness in change management.

Whereas Transition Reinforcement Skills depict HR's role in facilitating the change process, Transition Enabling skills are the ones which ensure that organisational members adapt successfully to the changes.

Transition reinforcement skills consist of four distinct subsets:

i. Analytical and Diagnostic skills, involving analysis of the context and the possible obstacles, etc;
ii. Administrative skills to understand and clarify how the change is linked to different HR systems and modify the same, if required.

iii. Process Implementation skills or the ability to facilitate the transition; and
iv. After care, for institutionalisation of changes.

Transition Enabling skills consist of two broad subsets:

i.   Provide support to employees in the process of accepting and institutionalising the changes and
ii. Provide support to line managers in their role as people managers and help them to appropriately address the reactions people and manage their expectations.

Proactiveness consists of two broad subsets:

i.   proactiveness in Culture Management, such as through bringing in appropriate HR practices, supporting new roles and responsibilities and celebrating success; and
ii. proactiveness in managing Incremental changes, by promoting improvisations, innovations and knowledge-sharing etc.

Influential Skills also consist of two broad categories:

i.   credibility of the HR Agents in establishing trust and demonstrating role model behaviour; and
ii. HR Change agents' leadership skills, to influence the organisational changes.

Competencies essentially signify the knowledge, attitudes, and behaviour that assist in bringing about performance outcomes. Having a competency framework in an organisation helps identify the competency gaps and helps prepare the necessary roadmap for linking the gaps with equivalent learning objects. HR Change Management competencies are considered as essential competencies in HR professionals which help them in discharging their essential role of ushering in desired change in an organisation.

HR Analytics

HRM service delivery during modern times is more personalised than ever before and HRM programs and practices vary across individuals in an organisation. Characterised by the adoption of artificial intelligence and advanced HR analytics, personalised HRM signifies providing tailored HR solutions and constitutes a subset of high-performance work practices (HPWPs) (Huang, Zhang, & Feng, 2020).

Analytics is the discipline which has grown at the inevitable intersection of engineering, computer science, decision making, and quantitative methods and it organises, examines and helps decipher the snowballing amounts of data, otherwise christened as big data, being produced by modern societies (Mortensen, Doherty, & Robinson, 2015). HR analytics can simply be understood as "the systematic application of predictive modelling using inferential statistics to existing HR people-related data in order to inform judgments about possible causal factors driving key HR-related performance indicators" (Edwards & Edwards, 2016, p. 2). From this perspective, HR analytics allow sophisticated statistics and quantitative analyses to be applied to make business activities more effective.

During modern times, data is big. Big data is too large for typical database tools to be able to capture, store, manage and analyse – an essentially subjective and flexible definition which ranges from 'a few dozen terabytes to multiple petabytes' (Manyika et al., 2011, p. 1). Another academic positioning has been to move the definition to the degree to which it delivers the material to conduct succinct analysis to explain and predict behaviour and outcomes (George, Haas & Pentland, 2014). Even as the former definition would focus solely on the entire gamut of unstructured data, including in emails, social networks, web contents, digital images, video footages, location data culled from smart phones and other electronic devices, etc., the latter one would focus on data mostly on existing Human Resource Information Systems, which is lesser by the standards of earlier defined unstructured data, but big, going by the quantitative data-sets resorted to in academic social science, and having ability to engender smart insights, by virtue of the longitudinal dimensions of the data.

HR Analytics includes statistics and research design. It extends beyond pervading identification and articulation of meaningful questions, gathering and using appropriate data from within and outside the HR function. It sets suitable standards for rigour and relevance and enhances the analytical competencies of HR throughout the organisation (Boudreau & Ramstad, 2004). There are a few questions that continue to appear in the literature around HR data analytics. These relate to 5Ws – what, why, who, where and when questions.

The **what** it is and what it is not debate is sought to be resolved by Davenport, Harris, and Shapiro (2010) by putting in place the range of applications that constitute 'talent analytics', from simplest 'human-capital facts' to most sophisticated analytics that help improve the 'talent supply chain'. HR analytics, thus, is defined as the "the application of a methodology and integrated process for improving the quality of people-related decisions for the purpose of improving individual and/or organisational performance" (Bassi, Carpenter, & McMurrer, 2010).

The **'why'** question stems from HR professionals' quest to prove HR's worth, by bringing in measurements to prove the value of the HR function. Boudreau and Ramstad summarize the problem clearly: "Understanding the returns and investments in HR programs and practices is useful, but the quest for ROI will not provide the entire solution to the need for a decision science...Most ROI calculations fail to change decisions about the vital human capital and organisation resources. They are used primarily to demonstrate the value of HR investments after the fact. ROI creates the wrong focus" (Boudreau & Ramstad, 2007, p. 192). The purpose of HR analytics is to improve individual and organisational performance, and HR Professionals should remain content at that.

Who will drive the future of HR analytics – the HR function or IT – for typically it is IT which owns the analytic software and tools necessary for HR analytics? Who will measure the financial impact of human capital – the HR function or the office of the CFO? There is no gainsaying that the people side of the business historically has not been a forte of either IT or finance. HR function needs to rise to the occasion by developing the skill sets, organisational capability and analytic wherewithal essential for leading HR analytics convincingly. In fact, HR professionals may have to be more data savvy and adopt increased analytical abilities, if they want to contribute effectively to the organisations in the future (Kryscynski, Reeves, Stice-Lusvardi, Ulrich, & Russell, 2018).

Finally, the questions, **'when** should the HR Analytics be used and **where**?' Is it plausible to make good global analytics in a world of diversified cultures, multifarious regulations and variegated standards? Or should HR analytics wait for evolution of truly one-size-fits all solutions? HR analytics offers the tools to bring fruition to the need for a single global solution. It provides the means to categorize with precision not only what is common across various environments (be it environmental or regulatory, etc.), but also that which is fraught with uniqueness due to local specifics.

Further, ethical questions about what the appropriate usage of HR analytics is and what it is not are raised, largely emanating from fast advances in software capability, coupled with snowballing capacity to pull together different pieces of information. Probably the best way to evade unforeseen ethical dilemmas is to create clearly spelt out and widely circulated principles for when HR analytics will and will not be used.

A Practical Road Map to Conducting HR Analytics

Mondore, Douthitt, and Carson (2011) have delineated a six-step process to ensure "HR analytics moves beyond conducting analysis and creates an environment of executive buy-in, cross-functional interaction, targeted initiative-building and a discipline of measurement and re-focusing" (p. 23).

Step 1: Determine Critical Outcomes

First determine the top two to three most critical outcomes of the change intervention that has been planned, so that the same could be focused on. For example, outcomes such as productivity, turnover and customer satisfaction are commonly desired outcomes – but those are not the end of the list. Financial indicators, costs and safety-related data are all results that can be linked to employees.

Step 2: Create Cross-Functional Data Team

Identify the various owners of the outcome data, who would become the key members of a cross-functional data team (CFDT). This CFDT may consist of expert statisticians, key business leaders or metric owners, and HR leadership. The statisticians are needed to determine data requirements, build scientific linkages between the datasets, and conduct the necessary statistical analyses.

Step 3: Assess Measures of Critical Outcomes

The next step is to determine how data are currently captured in the organisation. This step gets into the details of the actual analysis process, and evaluates realistically the utility of each outcome measure, such as frequency of measurement (e.g., monthly, quarterly, annually), level of measurement (e.g., by line of business, by work unit, by manager, at the store level, at the department/function level), or organisational owners of each of the outcome measures (e.g., the department or leader of the measurement), etc.

Step 4: Conduct Objective Analysis of Key Data

This part of the process will require advanced statistical knowledge to build requisite interconnections among the data, and may necessitate hiring a consultant, or outside expert. It would be important to establish cause-effect relationships for understanding how these different measures relate to each other as well as for establishing the organisational significance in terms of the change outcomes.

Step 5: Build the Program and Execute

Create interventions that will have the desired change effect. The big opportunity is that the investments should focus on those employee processes/skills/attitudes/demographics, that have been shown to have a direct impact on the organisation's desired business outcomes.

Step 6: Measure and Adjust/Re-prioritize

In the last step, re-measure to assess progress and calculate actual impact on the organisation. Like other organisational decisions, leaders need to make minor adjustments to initiatives along the way based on measurement results of the change outcomes.

Analytics has been pronounced a 'must have' competence for the HR profession; it is an instrument for creating value from individuals in the organisation and a means to increase the strategic effect of the HR function (CIPD, 2013). HR needs to act in tandem with other cross-functional data team members to bring in the desired change.

Participation of Employees in Decision Making Process

According to Boselie (2010), a high-performance work system comprises of specific HR practices that crafts employee competency, in terms of knowledge, skills and abilities and motivates employees and creates opportunities for them to participate in decision making. This explanation of Boselie is very close to what Bailey (1993) and Appelbaum and Berg (2001) have delineated in the AMO model. AMO is an acronym and it stands for A – Abilities, M – Motivation and O - Opportunity to Participate. Thus, work autonomy, decentralisation of decision-making, employee involvement in development and implementation of policies and teamwork constitute some of the salient points of HPWPs.

Management of employee participation has been pursued in many organisations. This is an attempt to make use of workers' creativity and skills, mainly in the managerial decision-making process (Durai, 2010). In some places, participation is conducted through periodic meetings at different structural levels of organisations. Over the years, participative decision–making (PDM) has become very prominent and consequently, academicians have also given attention to this topic (Irawanto, 2015).

Participative management is generally defined as a process in which there is influence-sharing among employees who are placed vertically in unequal hierarchical strata (Wagner, 1994). The practice of employees' participation in management balances the involvement of employees at senior and junior levels in the processing of information, decision making and problem solving. Thus, in a truncated connotation, employee participation is construed as "joint decision making or influence sharing between employees and managers" (Doucouliagos, 1995, p. 60). However, in a broader sense, participation is "a conscious and intended effort by individuals at a higher level in an organisation to provide visible extra-role or role-expanding opportunities for individuals or groups at a lower level in the organisation to have a greater voice in one or more areas of organisational performance" (Glew, O'Leary-Kelly, Griffin, & Van Fleet, 1995, p. 402).

Generally considered as the forerunners in the study of participatory management, Coch and French (1949) have espoused that there exists a direct connection between employees' participation in decision-making and increase of job satisfaction and productivity (Rooney, 1988). Likert (1961) has also observed that participatory decision-making can fulfil employees' need for self-actualisation and thus increase employees' motivation and performance outcomes. Studies have been made to examine relationship of participatory management to productivity (Levitan & Werneke, 1984), product quality (Cooke, 1992), reduction in absenteeism (Eaton & Voos, 1989), return on equity (Kim, Han, & Kim, 2017) and employee-superior relations (Posadzińska, Słupska, & Karaszewski, 2020); however, results have been ambivalent (Berdicchia & Masino, 2019; Ledford & Lawler, 1994; Wagner, 1994), because of usage of different methodologies.

In certain other studies, employee participation has been shown to lead to satisfaction (Cotton, Vollrath, Froggatt, Lengnick-Hall, & Jennings, 1988;). According to Blinder (1990), profit sharing programmes are more efficacious when implemented along with participatory management. Participatory decision-making could improve employee satisfaction with decisions made as well as with the process through which such decisions are made, thus solidifying both employees' commitment to such decisions, and their perception of justice meted out in the process (Cawley, Keeping, & Levy, 1998). This could lead to their heightened trust with the organisation (Nyhan, 2000).

The belief system a person may have about operational efficacy of participating in decision-making can be categorised into participation efficacy of self and collective participation efficacy. Studies have sought to explain self-efficacy (Bandura, 1997) and collective efficacy (Donohoo, Hattie, & Eells, 2018; Earley, 1994; Gist, 1987; Mischel & Northcraft, 1997; Riggs, Warka, Babasa, Betancourt, & Hooker, 1994). In the same vein, participation efficacy of self can be construed as the extent to which an individual believes that he or she has the knowledge, skills and ability to participate effectively in decision-making. Collective Participation efficacy is the extent to which members in the group trust that their group has the collective competencies to successfully participate in decision making. Theoretically, the effect of participatory decision-making on performance is a result of how employees use such instrumentality to create situations conducive to their effectiveness (Mitchell, 1973).

Employee participation in decision making in the organisational activities has become the key element in bringing successful implementation of new change management strategies within organisations. Participation augments motivation, ownership, and commitment to organisational change. Since participation results in emotional and mental fulfilment of employees, it helps in achieving the individual and organisational goals (Irawanto, 2015). When employees participate, they are also able to influence the working and decision-making of the organisation and their voice and work reaches the managerial decisions (George, 2011; Mannan, 1987). Participation improves the exchange of information and sharing of knowledge regarding what changes are to be made, so it is crucially required for superior decision making. In the process, individuals who are normally reticent and introverted and who may not share information during the normal course may get the desired motivation to do so. Participation is thus a two-way process – giving employees the opportunity to share their ideas and contribute to the change process and organisational development, while organisations benefit from the employees' ideas at the same time. In a nutshell, the twin factors of a climate of participation (Miller & Monge, 1986) and a feeling of having one's voice heard (Cawley et al., 1998) have a greater impact on employee satisfaction, thus facilitating smoother transitions during change management.

Spirituality, Ethics and Values

Several corporate scandals have marred the international business space over the years. A great fallout of the occurrence of such Corporate scandals has been a heightened cognition of the importance of spirituality, ethics and values in organisational life (Mishra, Shukla, & Sujatha, 2019).

Spirituality is that which comes from within (Turner, 1999) and so different people draw different connotations of it. Holistically, the self of individuals constitutes body, mind, emotions, and spirit, in totality. The interplay amongst individuals' spiritual yearnings, emotions, psychological capacity, and capability to learn are deeply interwoven (Howard, 2002). Spiritual reality is a unifying oneness (Howard, 2002). Mitroff and Denton (1999) say that spirituality is the basic acceptance that there is a superlative power, a being, and a force, in whatever manner one may christen it, that governs the entire universe. There is a purpose behind everything and everyone. Spirituality is also about being holistic, or being able to see that everything is interconnected with everything else (Zohar & Marshall, 2000). According to Moxley (1999), being spiritual is about being completely human, and about integrating all the energies that are parts of individuals.

Spiritual dimensions of life, couched with the values of self and selflessness, activate a positive difference towards 'Well Being' (Chan & Lew, 2005). For some, it has a religious connotation and for others it does not (Neck & Milliman, 1994). Turner (1999) says that one thing that spirituality is not, is 'organized religion'. Spirituality consists in an existential unification with a transcendental and revered entity (Hamidieh, 2018).

An increasing realisation of the unifying oneness of spiritualism has propelled organisations to incorporate the spiritual dimension – something that has less to do with rules and order and more with meaning, purpose, and a sense of community (Ashmos & Duchon, 2000). Benefiel (2003) labelled spirituality and organisational science as irreconcilable foes, but observed that "spirituality and management, once thought incompatible, have in the past decade fallen in love". Spirituality has inevitably crept into the workplace and businesses are turning inward in pursuit of a "soul", to foster creativity and inspire leaders (Galen & West, 1995).

Spirituality is about experiencing real purpose and meaning at work beyond pay checks and performance reviews (Marschke, Preziosi, & Harrington, 2011). These days many prospective employees give less priority to compensation and benefits than working in an ethical, value-oriented organisation where employees are not treated as mere cogs in the wheels, but essentially as human beings, having various levels of skills and competencies.

Workplace spirituality refers to the desire to do purposeful work that serves others. It involves longing for connectedness and wholeness (Ashar & Lane-Maher, 2004). White (2001) emphasizes that spirituality at work is becoming important because people want to feel connected to work that is important, and to each other at work. Spirituality is about people sharing and experiencing some common attachment, attraction, and togetherness with each other within their work unit and in the organisation as a whole (Hong, 2012). Spirituality fetches happiness and a sense of fulfilment in the employees. Personal fulfilment and high morale in turn usher in outstanding performance and lead to organisational success (Turner, 1999). Organisations have started to absorb that encouraging spirituality increases loyalty and augments morale (Ashmos & Duchon, 2000).

Spirituality in the workplace focuses on the needs of the employees and as a result better productivity is attained as valued employees, being better satisfied, tend to show better performance (Altaf & Awan, 2011. Employee spirituality has a direct linkage with intrinsic satisfaction which is derived from elements related to work itself, such as feelings of achievement, responsibility, advancement and growth (Herzberg, 1968).

A spiritual workplace inspires employees to be more creative, to adapt to changes more positively, and to attain better adjustments as they experience an augmented level of job satisfaction, psychological well-being, and organisational commitment (Martin, Jones, & Callan, 2005). Spirituality inevitably spawns creativity, which becomes the foundation of business success in an era where innovation is just a six-monthly advantage. According to Neck and Milliman (1994), spirituality can positively affect employee and organisational performance. It can lead individuals to experience consciousness at a deeper level, thereby increasing their intuitive abilities. This can help individuals develop a more purposeful and compelling organisational vision, which can increase innovation. Studies conducted by McLaughlin (1998) emphasize workplace spirituality as it increases the profitability of organisations by better performance.

The web of relationships at work manifests the mechanisms of the whole. Therefore, when spiritual individuals recognize that the survival, success, and well-being at work depend on their mutual dependence in a collaborative system, they move towards greater congruence and efficiency. The emerging desire to form a "community" within the culture demonstrates that teams and organisations that powerfully connect to their spirit, achieve exponential gains in products and services, and they find that work is sacred (White, 2001).

Johnson (2012) defines ethics as involving judgments about the rightness or wrongness of human behaviour. Ethical behaviour in business is "behaviour that is consistent with the principles, norms, and standards of business practice that have been agreed upon by society" (Trevino & Nelson, 2011. p. 19).

Commitment to ethics and performance outcomes are inextricably intertwined. Ethics, which draw the best in individuals, leaders, and the organisation, allow high performance to be carried out with commitment to values (Cantrell & Lucas, 2013). These days organisational ethics are taken as one of the most important components that move not only organisational efficiency, but organisational existence as well (Kwon Choi, Koo Moon, & Ko, 2013). An ethical work environment lies in shared perceptions of organisational practices that rivet on ethical content, and ethics and values command what a person should do (Victor & Cullen, 1988).

At the individual level, values can be defined as "one's core belief about what is important, what is valued, and how one should behave across a wide variety of situation" (Trevino & Nelson, 2011. p. 29). Organisational values, or core values, as they are sometimes christened, are like the signposts and provide direction to the way of life in the organisation. Core values are not a summation of individual values of all employees, but are common streaks, which cut across all such diverse values. These are the organisation's essential and enduring tenets – a small set of general guiding principles, which are understood, shared and endorsed by all.

Most organisations have between three to five such values, which are central to their collective identities (Johnson, 2012). Effective organisations identify and develop a clear, concise and shared meaning of values or beliefs, priorities, and direction, so that everyone understands and can contribute, once the defined values permeate every aspect of the organisation. The importance of organisational values has greatly increased in today's world of volatility and uncertainty, and values must be followed by every member of the organisation (Gupta, Kumar & Singh, 2014).

Research studies have demonstrated that the primary differentiator between successful companies and those which are not, has been whether they have had developed a core ideology and an envisioned future or not. In Built to Last, authors Collins and Porras (1997) offer a look at what makes visionary companies so outstanding and successful. To determine what makes the winners tick, they have taken 18 truly exceptional and long-lasting companies like General Electric, 3M, Merck, Wal-Mark, Walt Disney and Boeing and compared each one to a close competitor. For example, Sony is compared to Kenwood, Wal-Mart is compared to Ames and GE is compared to Westinghouse. Throughout, the authors have asked: 'What makes the truly exceptional companies different from other companies?' Drawing upon a six-year research project at the Stanford University Graduate School of Business, Collins and Porras, arrive at one of the conclusions that the great companies have outperformed the comparison companies because, among other things, they have taken pains to develop a Core Ideology (i.e., Core Values) and an Envisioned Future (i.e., Vision). According to a recent study by Watson Wyatt, companies whose employees understand the mission and goals enjoy a 29% greater return than other firms (Heathfield, 2017).

Milliman, Czaplewski, and Ferguson (2003) have found that organisational values are the most important spiritual factor at workplace. The importance of organisational values is also confirmed by Nordström and Riddersträle (2002), authors of the book Funky Business, who aver that "nowadays values determine loyalty" (p. 244).

Values and ethics mostly emanate from leaders and are disseminated to the lower sections of the employees. To have a competitive edge over other organisations, many of the leaders are now involved in building their organisations with values and ethics (Barclay, 2014). Some organisations use values "to shape the firm's strategy, its relationship to customers and to community" (Drazin, Hess, & Mihoubi, 2006, p. 9).

Researchers have quite often described HR's role as "custodian" of organisational values (Armstrong, 1995; Sadler, 1995; Torrington & Hall, 1995). According to Driscoll and Hoffman (1998) "HR as the ethics office isn't an oxymoron" and "Safeguarding the company is human resources' job". Wiley (1998) considers that HR has a role to play in being responsible for management of ethics. Caudron (1997, p. 63) has emphasised that "HR professionals must be able to understand and enforce ethical business behaviour". Kilcourse (1994) states that of all the C-suite employees, the human resource director has the largest responsibility to promote the company values and ethics. "By making explicit those values which drive the organisation" and "disseminating a list of clear ethical guidelines" (Kilcourse, 1994, p. 42), the HR director coaxes the other executives to internalise that the inculcation of ethical values is central for organisational success. Further, through appropriate HR systems, organisation can build an ethical climate (Jha, Varkkey, Agrawal, & Singh, 2017).

Spirituality, ethics and values are inextricably intermixed conceptualisations and are inevitably being emphasised for desired change management and organisational development for sustainability and growth.

Concluding Observations

High-performance work practices are generally categorised as organising work in a manner that will have a real impact on performance of individuals and organisations. Thus, the aim of HPWPs is to create an environment in which a level of performance becomes a way of life. Thus, HPWPs are some primary instrumentalities to bring in planned and desired change in organisations. Hence, a few of the HPWPs have been enunciated in this Chapter. The success of an organisation depends on its ability to measure accurately the performance of its members and use it objectively to optimize them as a vital resource (Pattanayak, 2009). According to Harel and Tzafrir (1999), the only HR variable that has had an impact on organisational performance is training and development, which in turn rivets on rigorous gap analysis for its success. HR Analytics is a developing discipline that can help enable HR to accomplish the promise of becoming a true strategic partner (Lawler III, Levenson, & Boudreau, 2004). Employee participation has been emphasised by many to augment performance, job satisfaction, and productivity in unison (Pfeffer, 1994; Verma, 1995; Wagner, 1994). In a theoretical study, Mishra, Shukla, and Sujatha (2019) propose that organisational ethics, values and moral standards, when practised, give concrete manifestation to augmentation of productivity and lead to growth, fruition of organisational objectives and long-term sustainability of the organisation.

Conclusions

If one examines the Fortune 500 list from 1955, i.e., the first year it was published, there are some companies that one would recognize, but many more have become extinct – dying of changes in their environment or being gobbled up by more aggressive carnivores. In fact, by the year 2017 only 60 companies out of the original list remained (Perry, 2017). Many foundered, shrivelled, grew outdated, or were acquired by competitors that became stronger. It is a Company-eat-Company world. If one doesn't change, one might as well perish. The history of the Corporate world is replete with examples of lost opportunities of erstwhile glaringly successful companies. A few elucidations would amply demonstrate this.

Cost of No-Changers

Blockbuster endured the evolution from Video Home System (VHS) to Digital Versatile Disc (DVD), but could not adapt to the next big wave of change. Netflix sent videos that the customers would have hired through Blockbuster straight to their homes, without due dates or late fees. Blockbuster remained flat-footed and unconcerned. Netflix eventually went from a mail-order facility to a streaming one and Blockbuster's orthodox retail outlets remained miserably outdated. On September 23, 2010 Blockbuster filed for bankruptcy. The company declared it would be ending its mail and retail store distribution centres in 2014, after it failed to adjust to the move towards streaming and kiosk rentals, aiming instead at impulse snack and toy purchases.

When IBM and Hewlett-Packard were selling most of their products through physical stores, Dell had the idea of cutting out the distributors and selling directly to consumers. On the emergence of the Internet, Dell ramped up its strategy and left its competitors way behind. A decade later, however, Dell faltered as mobile devices replaced

DOI: 10.4324/9781003191346-102

PCs, cheap Asian machines flooded the markets, and big customers started demanding end-to-end service, not just hardware. Dell tried to gain ground with mini-laptops, smartphones, and similar fashionable products, but then it was just following its competitors, and not leading the market (US News, 2010).

Borders Books launched its first store in Ann Arbor, Michigan in 1971 and had grown from strength to strength in 40 years. Borders, along with Barnes & Noble, had pioneered the book megastore business, but it could not change through the whirligig of time. When the world's reading habits changed to reading on phones, tablets or via the web, Borders did precious little to adopt any new technology. Borders re-launched its website in 2008, but it was too late. Borders focused on music sales of CDs and DVDs, when the industry was going digital (Vocoli, 2014). Barnes & Noble invested in beefing up its online sales and developed its own e-reader, the Nook. However, Borders expanded its plant, renovated its stores and outsourced its online sales operation to Amazon. It was finally liquidated in 2011, when almost 11,000 of its employees lost their jobs. However, Barnes & Noble survived.

Once Blackberry was at the helm of smartphone industry and it was the phone to have in the mid-to-late 2000s. In fact, in 2007 Blackberry had more than 50% of the market share of phones in the US. Then on June 29, 2007, the iPhone was released. Initially, Blackberry overlooked touch screen-based equipment, maintaining that their phones would continue to be the de-facto norm for enterprises. More so, as the iPhone initially wrangled with enterprise email security. By catching on to the imagination of consumer taste and slowly promoting Bring Your Own Device (BYOD) standards within companies, Apple redefined the market (Vocoli, 2014). Blackberry staggered, blinded by the shine of its own success. By 2014, Blackberry had 0.8% of the Smartphone market share, which dwindled to 0.0% by February 2017 (Intelligencer, 2017).

For nearly a century, no company in the photo camera industry was as successful as Kodak, whose innovations included the Brownie camera of 1900, the Kodachrome colour film, the handheld movie camera, and the easy-load Instamatic camera. Kodak's successful run of glory began to fade with the advent of digital photography (US News, 2010). Kodak missed out on the printers, software, file sharing, third-party apps and all that digital technology ushered in. Since the late 1980s, Kodak tried to expand into pharmaceuticals, memory chips, healthcare imaging, document management, and many other fields, but it could never reach its dizzy heights of success as with colour photo cameras. Kodak could not keep pace with the consumer trend from film to digital, and the once $31 billion company filed for bankruptcy in 2012.

In 2005, Yahoo owned 21% of the online advertising market and was number one among all players. However, by 2014, it was relegated to the number four position behind Google, Facebook and Microsoft. When web search and aggregation phenomena emerged, the ground-breaking Yahoo tried to charge for services like e-mail and file sharing, while upstart Google presented everything for free. Customers clustered around Google, which rushed to an enviable position in search that it still holds. Yahoo still developed into a huge Web portal, with coverage of sports, finance, and news, and it generates great income through advertising, but their desire to remain an online portal instead of a dominant search player led them to outsource their search engine to Microsoft Bing. They could not visualise the enormous portent of search and lost out on this opportunity (Vocoli, 2014).

Toys "R" Us thrived in the 1980s and 1990s, as its model of specialty megastores converged with a flood of American consumerism. As it grew in size to become Pan-American, Toys "R" Us drove many competitors out of business and devoured many. Then the winds of fortune changed its direction, and the toy giant got beaten by discounters like Wal-Mart and Target, online sites like Amazon, and smaller merchants with better quality and service. The company was bought in 2004 and the bid for turnaround resulted in closing of stores and large-scale layoffs and downsizing (US News, 2010).

American Suzuki Motor Corporation was founded in 1963 and was in the business of cars, trucks, scooters, all-terrain vehicles, sports utility vehicles, and marine engines. However, it's too-small cars didn't fit the large-and-in-charge American lifestyle through the changing times. As it failed to adapt its branding, the American Suzuki Motor Corporation filed for bankruptcy and on March 31, 2013 closed the sale of its operating assets to Suzuki Motor of America, Inc., which was a newly-organised, wholly-owned subsidiary of Suzuki Motor Corporation.

Myspace was born quickly and died too soon. A social networking website offering an interactive, user-submitted network of friends, personal profiles, blogs, groups, photos, music, and videos, from 2005 to 2008, Myspace was the largest social networking site in the world (Myspace, 2019) and in June 2006 beat Google to be reckoned as the most visited website in the United States. Facebook surpassed Myspace in April 2008 to be the most visited website among exclusive worldwide visitors. Among the reasons for the decline of Myspace is the fact that it got trapped to a portal strategy of building an audience around entertainment and music, whereas Facebook continually added new features to improve the social-networking experience. Facebook envisioned what Myspace could not: people need to link on multiple levels – through shared interests and groups and not just as casual bands trying to get signed.

As per Govindarajan and Trimble (2010), successful companies tend to fall into three traps. The first trap is the physical trap of big investments in erstwhile systems or equipment preventing the pursuit of more lucrative ones. The other two traps are the psychological trap of leaders' fixation on the model through which they have become successful and the strategic trap of focusing on the market of today and becoming oblivious to the future. This is what Ghoshal, Piramal, and Bartlett (2002) call the 'Ossification of Success'.

Thus, as one stretches open the rolled-up scrolls of the history of the business firmament, the story of lost opportunities comes out vividly. Successful companies get blinded by their own success, and the rigidities of their systems and processes results in 'ossification of success'. The current book has delved deep into the theoretical dimensions of change.

In Summary

The book has discussed diverse models of organisational strategy, different dimensions of changing business environment and implications for HR, various theories of organisational change, theories and dimensions of resistance to change, concepts such as Organisational Culture and Leadership Styles with respect to their interconnections with organisational change and puts in perspective the evolving role of HR. The book has also made an exposition of literature on High Performance Work Practices (HPWP) to support change management in organisations and literature on a few HPWPs, such as Performance Management and Feedback Mechanisms, Building Competencies, HR Analytics, Participation in Decision Making Process and Building Value-based organisations.

Limitations and Future Work

The scope of this book has been to make a theoretical exposition of what Organisational Change is and how organisations can prepare for change management. In today's Volatile, Uncertain, Complex and Ambiguous backdrop, organisations need to anticipate changes, prepare to face uncertainty and ambiguity as the goals of life and build competencies to tide over complexities. Changes in the business firmament through the changing times have led to several changes in the workplace, including its constituents, its structure and its processes (Mishra, Shukla, & Sujatha, 2017). The success of an organisation in the context of such change largely depends on HR's capability to develop appropriate and effective processes to manage such change. Change in business strategy has a lot of obligations for the Human Resources Function and its goings-on (Mishra et al., 2017). In this context of volatility, HR's role in creating, managing and institutionalising change needs careful scrutiny in the Indian context.

Hence, the book builds a theoretical foundation for other work of authors, which are to be based on rock-solid research by adopting both qualitative and quantitative methodologies. In this book, the authors build the theoretical edifice for scrutinising the role of HR as an instrument of change, to be taken up by them in their forthcoming books.

References

Abernathy, W. J., & Clark, K. B. (1985). Innovation: Mapping the winds of creative destruction. *Research Policy*, *14*(1), 3–22.

Ackerman, B. A. (1984). *Reconstructing American Law*. Boston, MA: Harvard University Press.

Ackerman, L. (1986). Development, transition or transformation: The question of change in organizations. *OD Practitioner*, *18*(4), 1–9.

Ackroyd, S., & Crowdy, P. A. (1990). Can culture -be managed? Working with "raw" material: The case of the English slaughtermen. *Personnel Review*, *19*(5), 3–13.

Adeniji, A. A., & Osibanjo, A. O., (2012). *Human Resource Management: Theory and Practice*. Lagos: Pumark Nigeria Limited.

Adobe, Great Place to Work. (2019). Extracted from https://www.greatplacetowork.in/great/rated/100-best/Adobe-India on 08.01.2021

Ahlstrom, D., & Bruton, G. D. (2009). *International Management: Strategy and Culture in the Emerging World*. Mason, OH: Cengage Learning.

Aldrich, H., & Mueller, S. (1982). The evolution of organisational forms-technology, coordination and control. *Research in Organizational Behavior*, *4*, 33–87.

Alford, R. (1975). *Health Care Politics*. London: University of Chicago Press.

Al-Mashari, M. (2003). A process change-oriented model for ERP application. *International Journal of Human-Computer Interaction*, *16*(1), 39–55.

Altaf, A., & Awan, M. A. (2011). Moderating affect of workplace spirituality on the relationship of job overload and job satisfaction. *Journal of Business Ethics*, *104*(1), 93–99.

Amabile, T. M., & Kramer, S. J. (2011). The power of small wins. *Harvard Business Review*, *89*(5), 70–80.

Andrews, K. R. (1971). *The Concept of Corporate Strategy*. New York: Dow Jones

Ansoff, H. (1965). *Corporate Strategy*. New York: Penguin Books.

Ansoff, H. I. (1987). *Corporate Strategy* (rev. ed.). New York: Penguin Books.

Antonelli, C. (2012). *New Information Technology and Industrial Change: The Italian Case*. New York: Springer Science & Business Media.

Appelbaum, E., & Berg, P. (2001). High-performance work systems and labor market structures. In E. Appelbaum & P. Berg (Eds.), *Sourcebook of Labor Markets* (pp. 271–293). Boston, MA: Springer.

Armenakis, A. A., Harris, S. G., & Mossholder, K. W. (1993). Creating readiness for organizational change. *Human Relations, 46*(6), 681–703.

Armstrong, M. (1995). *A Handbook of Personnel Management & Practice.* London: Kogan Page.

Armstrong, M. (2000). The name has changed, but has the game remained the same?. *Employee Relations, 22*(6), 576–593.

Armstrong, M. (2006). *A Handbook of Human Resource Management Practice.* London: Kogan Page Publishers.

Armstrong, M. (2009). *Armstrong's Handbook of Human Resource Management Practice* (11th ed.). New York: Kogan Page.

Armstrong, M., & Baron, A. (2005). *Managing Performance: Performance Management in Action.* London: CIPD Publishing.

Arogyaswamy, B., & Byles, C. M. (1987). Organizational culture: Internal and external fits. *Journal of Management, 13*(4), 647–658.

Ashar, H., & Lane-Maher, M. (2004). Success and spirituality in the new business paradigm. *Journal of management inquiry, 13*(3), 249–260.

Ashforth, B. E., & Lee, R. T. (1990). Defensive behavior in organizations: A preliminary model. *Human Relations, 43*, 621–648.

Ashforth, B. E., & Mael, F. A. (1998). The power of resistance: Sustaining valued identities. *In* R. M. Kramer & M. A. Neale (Eds.), *Power and Influence in Organizations* (pp. 89–120). Thousand Oaks, CA: Sage.

Ashmos, D. P., & Duchon, D. (2000). Spirituality at work: A conceptualization and measure. *Journal of Management Inquiry, 9*(2), 134–145.

Bailey, T. (1993). *Discretionary Effort and the Organization of Work: Employment Participation and Work Reform Since Hawthorne.* Teachers College and Conservation of Human Resources. New York: Columbia University.

Baird, L., & Meshoulam, I. (1988). Managing two fits of strategic human resource management. *Academy of Management Review, 13*(1), 116–128.

Baker, T. (1999). *Doing Well by Doing Good: The Bottom Line on Workplace Practices.* Washington, DC: Economic Policy Inst.

Balogun, J., & Hope Hailey, V. (2004). *Exploring Strategic Change* (2nd ed.). London: Prentice Hall.

Band, W.A. (1995). Making peace with change. *Security Management, 19*(3), 21–22.

Bandura, A. (1997). *Self-efficacy: The Exercise of Control.* New York: Freeman.

Baran, B. E., Filipkowski, J. N., & Stockwell, R. A. (2019). Organizational change: Perspectives from human resource management. *Journal of Change Management, 19*(3), 201–219.

Barclay, J. (2014). *Conscious Culture: How to Build a High Performing Workplace through Leadership, Values, and Ethics.* New York: Morgan James Publishing.

Barley, S. R. (1988). Technology, power, and the social organization of work: Towards a pragmatic theory of skilling and deskilling. *Research in the Sociology of Organizations, 6*, 33–80.

Barney, J. B. (1986). Strategic factor markets: Expectations, luck, and business strategy. *Management Science, 32*(10), 1231–1241.

Barney, J. B. (1991). Firm resources and sustained competitive advantage. *Journal of Management, 17*(1), 99–120.

Barney, J. B. (1992). Integrating organizational behavior and strategy formulation research: A resource based analysis. In P. Shrivastava, A. Huff & J. Dutton (Eds.), *Advances in Strategic Management*. Greenwich, CT: JAI Press.

Barney, J. B. (2002). Strategic management: From informed conversation to academic discipline. *Academy of Management Perspectives, 16*(2), 53–57.

Barney, J. B., & Wright, P. M. (1998). On becoming a strategic partner: The role of human resources in gaining competitive advantage. *Human Resource Management: Published in Cooperation with the School of Business Administration, The University of Michigan and in alliance with the Society of Human Resources Management, 37*(1), 31–46.

Bartlett, C. A., & Ghoshal, S. (2002). *Managing Across Borders: The Transnational Solution*. Boston, MA: Harvard Business Press.

Bartunek, J. M., & Moch, M. K. (1987). First-order, second-order, and third-order change and organization development interventions: A cognitive approach. *Journal of Applied Behavioral Science, 23*(4), 483–500.

Bass, B. M. (1985). *Leadership and Performance*. New York: Free Press.

Bass, B. M. (1990). From transactional to transformational leadership: Learning to share the vision. *Organizational Dynamics, 18*(3), 19–31.

Bass, B. M. (1999). Two decades of research and development in transformational leadership. *European Journal of Work and Organizational Psychology, 8*(1), 9–32.

Bassi, L. J., Carpenter, R., & McMurrer, D. (2010). *HR Analysis Handbook* (pp. 11, 13–14) Amsterdam: Reed Business.

Basu, K., & Palazzo, G. (2008). Corporate social responsibility: A process model of sensemaking. *Academy of Management Review, 33*(1), 122–136.

Bauer, T. N. (2010). Onboarding new employees: Maximizing success. *SHRM Foundation's Effective Practice Guideline Series*, Vol. 7. Alexandria, VA: SHRM Foundation.

Baum, H. S. (1987). *The invisible bureaucracy: The unconscious in organizational problem solving*. New York: Oxford University Press.

Baumgardner, A. H., Kaufman, C. M., & Levy, P. E. (1989). Regulating affect interpersonally: When low esteem leads to greater enhancement. *Journal of Personality and Social Psychology, 56*(6), 907–921.

Baumüller, M. (2007). Managing cultural diversity–An empirical examination of cultural networks and organizational structures as governance mechanisms in multinational corporations. *German Journal of Human Resource Management, 21*(4), 478–482.

Beach, S. D. (1980). *Personnel: The Management of People at Work.* New York: Macmillan Publishing Company.

Beck, A.T. (1988). *Love Is Never Enough.* New York, NY: Penguin Books.

Becker, B., & Gerhart, B. (1996). The impact of human resource management on organizational performance: Progress and prospects. *Academy of Management Journal, 39* (4), 779–802.

Becker, B. E., & Huselid, M.A. (1998). High performance work systems and farm performance: A synthesis of research and managerial implications. In G.R. Ferris (Ed.), *Research in Personnel and Human Resource Management* (pp. 53–101). Stamford, CT: JAI Press.

Becker, B. E., Huselid, M. A., & Ulrich, D. (2001). *The HR Scorecard: Linking People, Strategy, and Performance.* Boston, MA: Harvard Business School Press.

Beckhard, R., & Harris, R. T. (1977). *Organisational Transitions: Managing Complex Change.* Reading, MA: Addison-Wesley.

Beer, M., & Nohria, N. (Eds.). (2000). *Breaking the Code of Change* (Vol. 78, No. 3, pp. 133–141). Boston, MA: Harvard Business School Press.

Benefiel, M. (2003). Irreconcilable Foes? The Discourse of Spirituality and the Discourse of Organizational Science. *Organization, 10*(2), 383–391.

Benne, K. D., Chin, R., & Bennis, W. G. (1976). Science and practice. *The Planning of Change.* In W.G. Bennis, K.D. Benne, R. Chin, & K.E. Corey (Eds.), (3rd ed.). New York: Holt, Rinehart and Winston, 128–137.

Berdicchia, D., & Masino, G. (2019). The ambivalent effects of participation on performance and job stressors: The role of job crafting and autonomy. *Human Performance, 32*(5), 220–241.

Beugré, C. D. (2007). *A Cultural Perspective of Organizational Justice.* Charlotte: Information Age Publishing.

Bhatt, S. (2015). Prepare for the "uberisation" of business, says Maurice Lévy, Publicis. *The Economic Times.* Extracted from http://economictimes.indiatimes.com/magazines/brand-equity/prepare-for-the-uberisation-of-business-says-maurice-lvy-publicis/articleshow/48527810.cms on 23.01.2021.

Bjorkman, I., & Lu, Y. (2001). Institutionalization and bargaining power explanations of hrm practices in international joint ventures: the case of Chinese–Western joint ventures. *Organization Studies, 22*(3), 491–512.

Blau, P. M., Falbe, C. M., McKinley, W., & Tracy, P. K. (1976). Technology and organization in manufacturing. *Administrative Science Quarterly, 21,* 20–40.

Bleecker, S. (1994). The virtual organization. *Futurist, 28*(2), 29–39.

Blinder, A.S. (1990). *Paying for Productivity.* Washington, DC: Brookings.

Boon, C., Eckardt, R., Lepak, D. P., & Boselie, P. (2018). Integrating strategic human capital and strategic human resource management. *The International Journal of Human Resource Management, 29*(1), 34–67.

Bordia, P., Hunt, E., Paulsen, N., Tourish, D., & DiFonzo, N. (2004). Uncertainty during organizational change: Is it all about control?. *European Journal of Work and Organizational Psychology, 13*(3), 345–365.

Borman, W. C., & Motowidlo, S. M. (1993). Expanding the criterion domain to include elements of contextual performance. In SchmittN. & Borman W. C. (Eds.), *Personnel Selection in Organisations*(pp. 71–98). San Francisco, CA: Jossey-Bass.

Boselie, P. (2010). *Strategic Human Resource Management. A Balanced Approach.* London: McGraw-Hill Higher Education.

Boudreau, J. W., & Ramstad, P. M. (2004). Talentship and human resource measurement and analysis: From ROI to strategic organizatismional change. *Human Resource Planning, 29*, 25.

Boudreau, J. W., & Ramstad, P. M. (2007). *Beyond HR: The New Science of Human Capital.* Boston: Harvard Business Press.

Bourgeois III, L. J. (1984). Strategic management and determinism. *Academy of Management Review, 9*(4), 586–596.

Braun, W. H., & Warner, M. (2002). Strategic human resource management in western multinationals in China: The differentiation of practices across different ownership forms. *Personnel Review, 31*(5), 553–579.

Brockbank, W. (1999). If HR were really strategically proactive: Present and future directions in HR's contribution to competitive advantage. *Human Resource Management, 38*(4), 337–352.

Brower, R. S., & Abolafia, M. Y. (1995). The structural embeddedness of resistance among public managers. *Group & Organization Management, 20*(2), 149–166.

Bruce, J., & Lloyd, C. B. (1992). 13 Finding the ties that bind: Beyond headship and household. In Haddad L., Hoddinott J. & Alderman H. (Eds.), *Intrahousehold Resource Allocation in Developing Countries* (pp. 213–228). Baltimore, MD: Johns Hopkins University Press.

Bucăloiu, I., & Tănăsescu, I. A. (2019). Correlations between the process of the organisational change and the characteristics of a communicating organisation. *Annals of Constantin Brancusi'University of Targu-Jiu. Economy Series, 3*, 136–142.

Budhwar, P., Luthar, H., & Bhatnagar, J. (2006). Dynamics of HRM systems in BPOs operating in India. *Journal of Labour Research, 27*(3), 339–360.

Budhwar, P., & Sparrow, P. (2002). An integrative framework for determining cross-national human resource management practices. *Human Resource Management Review, 12*(3), 377–403.

Burke, W. (1994). *Organization Development: A Process of Learning and Changing* (2nd ed.). Reading, MA: Addison-Wesley.

Burnes, B. (2004). *Managing Change: A Strategic Approach to Organisational Dynamics*, (4th ed.). Harlow: Prentice Hall.

Burns, J. M. (1978). *Leadership.* New York: Harper and Raw.

Burns, D. D. (1990). *The Feeling Good Handbook.* New York: Plume/Penguin Printing.

Burns, T., & Stalker, G. M. (1961). *The Management of Innovation.* London: Tavistock.

Butler, J. E., Ferris, G. R., & Napier, N. K. (1991). *Strategy and Human Resource Management*. Cincinnati, OH: South-Western Publishing.

Cable, D. M., & Judge, T. A. (1994). Pay preferences and job search decisions: A person-organization fit perspective. *Personnel Psychology, 47*(2), 317–348.

Cairncross, F. (2001). *Death of Distance: How The Communications Revolution is hanging Our Lives*. Boston, MA: Harvard Business School.

Caldwell, R. (2003). The changing roles of personnel managers: old ambiguities, new uncertainties. *Journal of Management Studies, 40*(4), 983–1004.

Cameron, E., & Green, M. (2009). *Making Sense of Change Management* (2nd ed.). Philadelphia: Kogan Page.

Campbell, J. P. (1990). Modelling the performance prediction problem in industrial and organisational Psychology. In M. D. Dunnette & L. M. Hough (Eds.), *Handbook of Industrial and organisational Psychology* (pp. 687–732). Palo Alto, CA: Consulting Psychologists Press.

Cantrell, W., & Lucas, J. R. (2013). *High-Performance Ethics: 10 Timeless Principles for Next-Generation Leadership*. Carol Stream: Tyndale House Publishers, Inc.

Cappelli, P., & Neumark, D. (2001). Do "high-performance" work practices improve establishment-level outcomes?. *Industrial and Labor Relations Review, 54*(4), 737–775.

Carnall, C. A. (1986). Toward a theory for the evaluation of organizational change. *Human Relations, 39*(8), 745–766.

Carnall, C. A. (2003). *Managing Change in Organizations* (4th ed.). Harlow: Prentice Hall.

Carter, N. M. (1984). Computerization as a predominate technology: Its influence on the structure of newspaper organizations. *Academy of Management Journal, 27*(2), 247–270.

Caudron, S. (1997). World-class executives. *Industry Week, 246*(22), 60–66.

Cawley, B. D., Keeping, L. M., & Levy, P. E. (1998). Participation in the performance appraisal process and employee reactions: A meta-analytic review of field investigations. *Journal of applied psychology, 83*(4), 615.

Chan, K. Y., & Lew, P. (2005). The challenge of systematic leadership development in the Singapore Armed Forces. *Journal of the Singapore Armed Force, 30*(4).

Chandler, A. (1962). *Strategy and Structure*. Cambridge: MIT Press.

Chandler, A. D. (1992). Organizational capabilities and the economic history of the industrial enterprise. *Journal of Economic Perspectives, 6*(3), 79–100.

Chartered Institute for Personnel and Development (CIPD). (2013). Talent analytics and big data—The challenge for HR.

Chawla, A., Sujatha, R., & Shukla, B. (2016). Demystifying leadership-regular and intelligible sequence of essentials discernible in the way in which something happens or is done. *Global Journal of Management And Business Research, 16*(4).

Child, J. (1994). *Management in China during the Age of Reform*. Cambridge: Cambridge University Press.

Child, J., & Smith, C. (1987). The context and process of organisational transformation – Cadbury limited in its sector. *Journal of Management Studies, 24*(6), 565–593.

Choi, M. (2011). Employees' attitudes toward organizational change: A literature review. *Human Resource Management, 50*(4), 479–500.

Choi, M., & Ruona, W. E. (2011). Individual readiness for organizational change and its implications for human resource and organization development. *Human Resource Development Review, 10*(1), 46–73.

Chung, B. (2007). *An analysis of success and failure factors for ERP systems in engineering and construction firms* (Doctoral dissertation, University of Maryland).

Ciborra, C. U., & Lanzara, G. F. (1991). Designing networks in action: formative contexts and post-modern systems development. In R. Clarke and J. Cameron (eds.) *Managing Information Technologies Organisational Impact* (pp. 265–279). Amsterdam, Holland: Elsevier Science Publishers.

Cimini, C., Boffelli, A., Lagorio, A., Kalchschmidt, M., & Pinto, R. (2020). How do industry 4.0 technologies influence organisational change? An empirical analysis of Italian SMEs. *Journal of Manufacturing Technology Management, 32*(3), pp. 695–721.

CISCO, Great Place to Work (2019). Extracted from https://www.greatplacetowork.in/great/rated/100-best/Cisco-Systems-India-Pvt-Ltd on 08.01.2021.

Clampitt, P., & Berk, L. R. (1996). Strategically communicating organisational change. *Jounral of Communication Management, 1*(1), 15–28.

Cloud computing. (2021). Extracted from https://www.investopedia.com/terms/c/cloud-computing.asp on 23.01.2021.

Coch, L., & French Jr., J. R. (1949). Overcoming Resistance. *Human Relations, 1*(4), 512–533.

Coetsee, L. (1999). From resistance to commitment. *Public Administration Quarterly, 23*(2), 204–222.

Coghlan, D. (1993). A person-centred approach to dealing with resistance to change. *Leadership & Organization Development Journal, 14*(4), 10–14.

Coghlan, D., & Rashford, N. S. (1990). Uncovering and dealing with organisational distortions. *Journal of Managerial Psychology, 5*(3),17–21.

Colbert, B. A. (2004). The complex resource-based view: Implications for theory and practice in strategic human resource management. *Academy of Management Review, 29*(3), 341–358.

Collins, D. (2005). *Organisational Change: Sociological Perspectives.* London: Routledge.

Collins, J. C., & Porras, J. I. (1997). *Built to Last: Successful Habits of Visionary Companies.* New York: Harper Business.

Colville, K., & Millner, D. (2011). Embedding performance management: Understanding the enablers for change. *Strategic HR Review, 10*(1), 35–40.

Conner, K. R. (1991). A historical comparison of resource-based theory and five schools of thought within industrial organization economics: Do we have a new theory of the firm?. *Journal of Management, 17*(1), 121–154.

Conner, J., & Ulrich, D. (1996). Human resource roles: Creating value, not rhetoric. *People and Strategy, 19*(3), 38–50.

Cooke, W. N. (1992). Product quality improvement through employee participation: The effects of unionization and joint union-management administration. *Industrial & Labor Relations Review, 46*(1), 119–134.

Cooke, F. L. (2004). Foreign firms in China: Modelling HRM in a toy manufacturing corporation. *Human Resource Management Journal, 14*(3), 31–52.

Corey, G. (1996). *Theory and Practice of Counselling and Psychotherapy* (5th ed.). Pacific Grove, CA: Brooks.

Cotton, J. L., Vollrath, D. A., Froggatt, K. L., Lengnick-Hall, M. L., & Jennings, K. R. (1988). Employee participation: Diverse forms and different outcomes. *Academy of Management Review, 13*(1), 8 – 22.

Crandall, N. F., & Wallace Jr, M. J. (1997). Inside the virtual workplace: Forging a new deal for work and rewards. *Compensation & Benefits Review, 29*(1), 27–36.

Crook, T. R., Todd, S. Y., Combs, J. G., Woehr, D. J., & Ketchen Jr, D. J. (2011). Does human capital matter? A meta-analysis of the relationship between human capital and firm performance. *Journal of applied psychology, 96*(3), 443.

Crozier, M. (1964). *The Bureaucratic Phenomenon*. London: Tavistock.

Cummings, T. G., & Huse, E. F. (1989). *Organization Development and Change* (4th ed.). St Paul, MN: West Publishing.

Cummings, T. G., & Worley, C. G. (2009). *Organizational Development and Change*. Mason, OH: South Western Cangage Learning.

Cunningham, J. B., & Kempling, J. S. (2009). Implementing change in public sector organizations. *Management Decision, 47*(2), 330–344.

Daley, J. (2010). Tearing down the walls: How social media is changing everything about the way we do business. *Entrepreneur, 56*.

Damanpour, F., & Schneider, M. (2008). Characteristics of innovation and innovation adoption in public organizations: Assessing the role of managers. *Journal of Public Administration Research and Theory, 19*(3), 495–522.

Dambra, L., & Potter, S. (1999). *The virtual organization.*

Darling, P. (1993). Getting results: The trainer's skills. *Management Development Review, 6*(5), 25–29.

Davenport, T. H. (1998). Putting the enterprise into the enterprise system. *Harvard business review, 76*(4). 121–131.

Davenport, T. H., Harris, J., & Shapiro, J. (2010). Competing on talent analytics. *Harvard Business Review, 88*(10), 52–58.

Davidow, W., & Malone, M. (1992). *The virtual corporation: Structuring and revitalizing the corporation for the 21st century*. New York: Harpers.

Dawson, P. (1994). *Organizational Change: A Processual Approach*. London: Paul Chapman Publishing.

Deal, T. E. (1985). Culture change: Opportunity, silent killer, or metamorphosis?. In R.H. Kilmann, M. J. Saxton, & R. Serpa, (Eds.), *Gaining Control of the Corporate Culture*. San Francisco, CA: Jossey-Bass.

Deal, T. E., & Kennedy, A. A. (1982). Corporate cultures: The rites and rituals of organizational life. *Reading/T. Deal, A. Kennedy.–Mass: Addison-Wesley*, 2, 98–103.

de La Cruz Paragas, F., & Lin, T. T. (2016). Organizing and reframing technological determinism. *New Media & Society, 18*(8), 1528–1546.

Delaney, J. T., & Goddard, J. (2001). An industrial relations perspective on the high-performance paradigm. *Human Resource Management Review, 11*(4), 395–429.

Delery, J. E., & Doty, D. H. (1996). Modes of theorizing in strategic human resource management: Tests of universalistic, contingency, and configurational performance predictions. *Academy of Management Journal, 39*(4), 802–835.

Deming, W. E. (1986). *Out of the Crisis.* Cambridge, MA: MIT Press.

Denis, J. L., Lamothe, L., & Langley, A. (2001). The dynamics of collective leadership and strategic change in pluralistic organizations. *Academy of Management Journal, 44* (4), 809–837.

Denison, D. (1990). *Corporate Culture and Organizational Effectiveness.* New York: Wiley.

Dent, E. B., & Goldberg, S. G. (1999). Challenging "resistance to change." *The Journal of Applied Behavioral Science, 35*(1), 25–41.

Devanna, M. A., Fombrun, C. J., & Tichy, N. M. (1984). A Framework for Strategic Human Resource Management. In C. J. Fombrun, N. M. Tichy & Devanna, M. A. (Eds.), *Strategic Human Resource Management.* New York: John Wiley and Sons.

DeVries, D. L., Morrison, A. M., Shullman, S. L., & Gerlach, M. L. (1981). *Performance Appraisal on the Line.* Greensboro, NC: Center for Creative Leadership.

Digital initiatives (2017). Extracted from https://www.ntpc.co.in/en/media/press- releases/details/digital-initiative-begins-ntpc-towards-paperless-office on 08.01.2021

DiMaggio, P., & Powell, W. (1983). The iron cage revisited: Institutional isomorphism and collective rationality in organizational fields. *American Sociological Review, 48*(2), 147–160.

Donohoo, J., Hattie, J., & Eells, R. (2018). The power of collective efficacy. *Educational Leadership, 75*(6), 40–44.

Doucouliagos, C. (1995). Worker participation and productivity in labor-managed and participatory capitalist firms: A meta-analysis. *Industrial and Labor Relations Review, 49*(1), 58 – 77.

Draganidis, M., & Mentzas, G. (2006). Competency based management: A review of systems and approaches. *Information Management & Computer Security, 14*(1), 51–64.

Drake, B. H. & Drake, E. (1988). *Ethical and legal aspects of managing corporate cultures. California Management Review, 30*(2), 107–123.

Drazin, R., Hess, E. D., & Mihoubi, F. (2006). Synovus Financial Corporation: "Just take care of your people". In E. D. Hess & K. S. Cameron (Eds.),

Leading with Values: Positivity, Virtue and High Performance. Cambridge: Cambridge University Press.

Driscoll, D. M., & Hoffman, W. M. (1998). HR plays a central role in ethics programs. *Workforce, 77*(4), 121–123.

Du Plessis, A. J. (2009). An overview of the influence of globalisation and internationalisation on domestic Human Resource Management in New Zealand. *International Review of Business Research Papers, 5*(2), 1–18.

Dunphy, D. C., & Stace, D. A. (1988). Transformational and Coercive Strategies for Planned Organizational Change. *Organizational Studies, 9*(3), 317–334.

Dunphy, D. C., & Dick, R. (1989). *Organizational Change by Choice*. Sydney: McGraw Hill Book Company.

Dunphy, D., & Stace, D. (1993). The strategic management of corporate change. *Human Relations, 46*(8), 905–920.

Durai, P. (2010). *Human Resource Management*. New Delhi: Pearson Education India.

Dyer, L., & Reeves, T. (1995). Human resource strategies and firm performance: What do we know and where do we need to go?. *The International Journal of Human Resource Management, 6*(3), 656–670.

Dyer, J. H., & Singh, H. (1998). The relational view: Cooperative strategy and sources of interorganisational competitive advantage. *The Academy of Management Review, 23*(4), 660–679.

Earley, P. C. (1994). Self or group? Cultural effects of training on self-efficacy and performance. *Administrative Science Quarterly, 39*, 89 – 117.

Eaton, A. E., & Voos, P. B. V. (1989). *Unions and contemporary innovations in work organization, compensation, and employee participation*. Kingston: Industrial Relations Centre, Queen's University.

Edwards, M. R., & Edwards, K. (2016). *Predictive HR Analytics: Mastering the HR Metric*. London: Kogan Page Publishers.

Edwards, H. M., & Humphries, L. P. (2005). Change management of people and technology in an ERP implementation. *Journal of Cases on Information Technology, 7*(4), 144–161.

Em360.(2018). Extracted from https://em360tech.com/tech-news/top-ten/top-10- companies-supporting-bring-device-culture on 08.01.2021

Epstein, M. J., & Roy, M. J. (2003). Making the business case for sustainability: linking social and environmental actions to financial performance. The *Journal of Corporate Citizenship, 9*(1), 79–96.

Escher, M. C. (1986). *Escher on Escher: Exploring the Infinite*. New York: Harry N. Abrams Inc.

Essentials, H. B. (2005). *Strategy: Create and Implement the Best Strategy for Your Business*. Boston, MA: Harvard Business School.

Essentials, H. B. (2006). D*ecision making–5 steps to better results*. Boston, MA: Harvard Business School Publishing.

Evans, R. (1994). The human side of business process re-engineering. *Management Development Review, 7*(6), 10–12.

Expenses Uber, Uber Alles, Gulliver, Business Travel, *The economist* (2015, March 11). Extracted from https://www.economist.com/gulliver/2015/03/11/uber-uber-alles on 23.01.2021.

Explained: What is 5G. (2021). Extracted from https://indianexpress.com/article/explained/what-is-5g-and-how-prepared-is-india-to-adapt-to-this-tech-7150641/ on 23.01.2021

Farley, J. U., Hoenig, S., & Yang, J. Z. (2004). Key factors influencing HRM practices of overseas subsidiaries in China's transition economy. *International Journal of Human Resource Management, 15*(4-5), 688–704.

Faupel, S., & Süß, S. (2019). The effect of transformational leadership on employees during organizational change–an empirical analysis. *Journal of Change Management, 19*(3), 145–166.

Ferner, A., & Quantanilla, J. (1998). Multinationals, national business systems and HRM: The enduring influence of national identity or a process of 'Anglo-Saxonization. *International Journal of Human Resource Management, 9*(4), 710–731.

Fey, C. F., Bjo¨rkman, I., & Pavlovskaya, A. (2000). The effect of human resource management practices on firm performance in Russia. *International Journal of Human Resource Management, 11*(1), 1–18.

Fillion, G., Koffi, V., & Ekionea, J. P. B. (2015). Peter Senge's learning organization: A critical view and the addition of some new concepts to actualize theory and practice. *Journal of Organizational Culture, Communications and Conflict, 19*(3), 73.

Fitzgerald, L., & Moon, P. (1996). *Performance Measurement in Service Industries: Making It Work.* London: The Chartered Institute of Management Accountants.

Fitzgerald, L., Johnston, R., Brignall, T. J., Silvestro, R., & Voss, C. (1991). Performance measurement in service businesses. *Management Accounting, 69*(10), 34–36.

Flamholtz, E. G., & Randle, Y. (1998). *Changing the Game: Organizational Transformation of the First, Second, and Third Kinds.* New York: Oxford University Press.

Folger, R., & Skarlicki, D. P. (1999). Unfairness and resistance to change: Hardship as mistreatment. *Journal of Organizational Change Management, 12*(1), 35–50.

Folkman, S., Lazarus, R. S., Gruen, R. J., & DeLongis, A. (1986). Appraisal, coping, health status, and psychological symptoms. *Journal of Personality and Social Psychology, 50,* 571–579.

Ford, J. D., & Ford, L. W. (2009). Decoding resistance to change. *Harvard Business Review, 87*(4), 99–103.

Fox, S., & Amichai-Hamburger, Y. (2001). The power of emotional appeals in promoting organizational change programs. *The Academy of Management Executive, 15*(4), 84–94.

Fransman, M. (1999). *Visions of Innovation -- The Firm and Japan.* Oxford: Oxford University Press.

Furst, S. A., & Cable, D. M. (2008). Employee resistance to organizational change: Managerialinfluence tactics and leader-member exchange. *Journal of Applied Psychology, 93*(2), 453.

Galbraith, J. R. (1973). *Designing Complex Organizations*. Reading, MA: Addison-Wesley.

Galen, M., & West, K. (1995). Companies hit the road less traveled. *Business Week, 6*(5), 95.

Garavan, T. N., Costine, P., & Heraty, N. (1995). The emergence of strategic human resource development. *Journal of European Industrial Training, 19*(10), 4–10.

Garg, N. (2019). High performance work practices and organizational performance-mediation analysis of explanatory theories. *International Journal of Productivity and Performance Management,68*(4). 797–816.

Gecas, V. (1982). The Self-concept. *Annual Review of Sociology, 8*(1), 1–33.

George, O. J. (2011). *Impact of Culture on the Transfer of Management Practices in Former British Colonies: A Comparative Case Study of Cadbury (Nigeria) Plc and Cadbury Worldwide*. London: Xlibris Corporation.

George, G. Haas, M., & Pentland, A. (2014). Big data and management. *Academy of Management Journal, 57*(2), 321 – 326.

Gerhart, B., Wright, P. M., McMahan, G. C., & Snell, S. A. (2000). Measurement error in research on human resources and firm performance: How much error is there and how High and Low Road Approaches to the Management of Human Resources does it influence effect size estimates?. *Personnel Psychology, 53*(4), 803–834.

Gersick, C. J. (1991). Revolutionary change theories: A multilevel exploration of the punctuated equilibrium paradigm. *Academy of Management Review, 16*(1), 10–36.

Ghoshal, S., Piramal, G., & Bartlett, C. A. (2002). *Managing radical change: What Indian companies must do to become world-class*. India: Penguin Books.

Giangreco, A. (2002). *Conceptualisation and operationalisation of resistance to change*. Italy: Libero Istituto Universitario Carlo Cattaneo.

Giangreco, A., & Peccei, R. (2005). The nature and antecedents of middle manager resistance to change: Evidence from an Italian context. *International Journal of Human Resource Management, 16*(10), 1812–1829.

Gist, M. E. (1987). Self-efficacy: Implications for organizational behaviour and human resource management. *Academy of Management Review, 12*(3), 472 – 485.

Gist, M. E., Schwoerer, C., & Rosen, B. (1989). Effects of alternative training methods on self-efficacy and performance in computer software training. *Journal of Applied Psychology, 74*(6), 884–891.

Glaister, K. W., & Falshaw, J. R. (1999). Strategic planning still going strong. *Long Range Planning, 32*(1),107–116.

Glaister, A. J., Karacay, G., Demirbag, M., & Tatoglu, E. (2018). HRM and performance—The role of talent management as a transmission mechanism in an emerging market context. *Human Resource Management Journal,* *28*(1), 148–166.

Glew, D. J., O'Leary-Kelly, A. M., Griffin, R. W., & Van Fleet, D. D. (1995). Participation in organizations: A preview of the issues and proposed framework for future analysis. *Journal of Management, 21*(3), 395–421.

Goldberg, L. R. (1992). The development of markers for the big-five factor structure. *Psychological Assessment, 4*(1), 26–42.

Golden, K. A., & Ramanujam, V. (1985). Between a dream and a nightmare: On the integration of the human resource management and strategic business planning process. *Human Resource Management, 24*(4), 429–452.

Gomez-Mejia, L. R., & Balkin, D. B. (1989). Effectiveness of individual and aggregate compensation strategies. *Industrial Relations, 28*(3), 431–445.

Goodenough, M., (2013). Cloud Computing: Effectively Changing The Business Operation Model. *Forbes.* Extracted from https://www.forbes.com/sites/centurylink/2013/05/16/cloud-computing-effectively-changing-the-business-operation-model/?sh=23676a0820e2 on 23.01.2021.

Govindarajan, V., & Trimble, C. (2010). *The Other Side of Innovation: Solving the Execution Challenge.* Boston, MA: Harvard Business Press.

Gowan, M. (2001). *E-HRM: An Internet Guide to Human Resource Management.* United States: Pearson.

Graetz, F. (2000). Strategic change leadership. *Management Decision, 38*(8), 550–562.

Grant, R. M., & Baden-Fuller, C. (1995, August). A knowledge-based theory of inter-firm collaboration. In *Academy of management proceedings (Vol. 1995,* No. 1, pp. 17–21). Briarcliff Manor, NY: Academy of Management.

Greengard, S. (2001). Make smarter business decisions: Know what employees can do. *Workforce, 80*(11), 42–45.

Gregory, K. L. (1983). Native-view paradigms: Multiple cultures and culture conflicts in organizations. *Administrative Science Quarterly, 28*(3), 359–376.

Greif, A. (2006). *Institutions and the Path to the Modern Economy: Lessons from Medieval Trade.* Cambridge, UK: Cambridge University Press.

Grieves, J. (2003). *Strategic Human Resource Development.* Thousand Oaks, CA: Sage.

Griffin, R. W. (2006). *Management* (8th ed.). Boston, MA: Houghton Mifflin Company.

Guest, D. E. (1997). Human resource management and performance: A review and research agenda. *International Journal of Human Resource Management, 8*(3), 263–276.

Guest, D. E., & Peccei, R. (2001). Partnership at work: Mutuality and the balance of advantage. *British Journal of Industrial Relations, 39*(2), 207–236.

Guest, D. E., Michie, J., Conway, N., & Sheehan, M. (2003). Human resource management and corporate performance in the UK. *British Journal of Industrial Relations, 41*(2), 291–314.

Gupta, M., Kumar, V., & Singh, M. (2014). Creating satisfied employees through workplace spirituality: A study of the private insurance sector in Punjab (India). *Journal of Business Ethics, 122*(1), 79–88

Haberberg, A. (2000). Swatting Swot. *Strategy (Strategic Planning Society)* (September).

Hackman, T. (2017). Leading change in action: Reorganizing an academic library department using Kotter's eight stage change model. *Library Leadership and Management, 31*(2).

Hage, J., & Aiken, M. (1970). *Social Change in Complex Organizations.* New York, NY: Random House.

Hamel, G., & Prahalad, C. K. (1994). Competing for the Future. *Harvard Business Review, 72*(4), 122–128.

Hamid, R., Ali, S. S., Reza, H., Arash, S., Ali, N. H., & Azizollah, A. (2011). The analysis of organizational diagnosis on based six box model in universities. *Higher Education Studies, 1*(1), 84–92.

Hamidieh, B. (2018). A Probe about the nuances between spirituality and religion. *Journal of Religious Studies, 11*(22), 79–106.

Hammer, M., & Champy, J. (1993). *Reengineering the Corporation.* New York: Harper Collins.

Hannan, M. T., & Freeman, J. (1989). *Organizational Ecology.* Cambridge, MA: Harvard University Press.

Hannan, M. T., & Carroll, G. R. (1992). *Dynamics of Organizational Populations –Density, Legitimation, and Competition.* Oxford: Oxford University Press.

Harel, G. H., & Tzafrir, S. S. (1999). The effect of human resource management practices on the perceptions of organizational and market performance of the firm. *Human Resource Management: Published in Cooperation with the School of Business Administration, The University of Michigan and in alliance with the Society of Human Resources Management, 38*(3), 185–199.

Harper, S. C. (2011). *The Ever-Evolving Enterprise: Guidelines for Creating Your Company's Future.* Santa Barbara: ABC-CLIO.

Hatch, M. J. (1997). *Organization Theory: Modern, Symbolic and Postmodern Perspectives.* Oxford: Oxford University Press.

Heathfield, S.M. (2017). Building a Strategic framework. Extracted from https://www.thebalance.com/build-a-strategic-framework-through-strategic-planning-1916834 on 23.01.2021.

Heilbroner, R. L. (1967). Do Machines Make History?. *Technology and Culture, 8*(3), 335–345.

Hendrickson, S., & Gray, E. J. (2012). Legitimizing resistance to organizational change: A social work social justice perspective. *International Journal of Humanities and Social Science, 2*(5), 50–59.

Hendry, C. (1996). Understanding and creating whole organizational change through learning theory. *Human Relations, 49*(5), 621–641.

Heneman, R. L., & Thomas, A. L. (1997). The Limited Inc.: Using strategic performance management to drive brand leadership. *Compensation and Benefits Review, 27*(6), 33–40.

Herold, D. M., Fedor, D. B., Caldwell, S., & Liu, Y. (2008). The effects of transformational and change leadership on employee's commitment to a change: a multilevel study. *Journal of Applied Psychology, 93*(2), 346–357.

Herzberg, F. (1968). One more time: How do you motivate employees? In S. J. Ott (Ed.), *Classical Readings in Organizational Behavior*. Orlando, Fl: Harcourt Brace & Company.

Hickson, D. J. (1985). *Top Decisions: Strategic Decision Making in Organisations*. San Francisco, CA: Jossey-Bass.

Hinings, C. R., & Greenwood, R. (1989). *The Dynamics of Strategic Change*. Oxford: Basil Blackwell.

Hitt, M., Ireland, R. D., & Hoskisson, R. (2009). *Strategic Management Cases: Competitiveness and Globalization*. London: Cengage Learning.

Hjalmarsson, A. K., & Dåderman, A. M. (2020). Relationship between emotional intelligence, personality, and self-perceived individual work performance: A cross-sectional study on the Swedish version of TEIQue-SF. *Current Psychology*, 1–16. https://doi.org/10.1007/s12144-020-00753-w

Hong, Y. J. (2012). Identifying spirituality in workers: A strategy for retention of community mental health professionals. *Journal of Social Service Research, 38* (2), 175–186.

Hooley, G., Cox, T., Shipley, D., Fah, J., Breaks, J., & Kilos, K. (1996). Foreign direct investment in Hungary: resource acquisition and domestic competitive advantage. *Journal of International Business Studies, 27*(4),683–709.

Howard, S. (2002). Spiritual perspective on learning in the work place. *Journal of Management Psychology, 17* (3), 230–243.

Huang, X., Zhang, L., & Feng, C. (2020). Personalized human resource management: Theory and implications. In *Academy of Management Proceedings* (*Vol. 2020*, No. 1, p. 12029). New York: Academy of Management.

Hummel, R. (1982). *The Bureaucratic Experience* (2nd ed.). New York: St. Martin's Press.

Huselid, M. A. (1995). The impact of human resource management on turnover, productivity, and corporate performance. *Academy of Management Journal, 38*(3), 635–672.

Hutchins, E. (1991). Organizing work by adaptation. *Organization Science, 2*(1), 14–39.

Ihlenburg, F. (2019). Diversity management and practical wisdom: Organizational change success factors. In *Practical Wisdom and Diversity* (pp. 189–204). Springer Gabler, Wiesbaden.

Ihsani, R. K., & Syuhada, M. N. (2020). Organizational Development with Six-Box Weisbord's Diagnostic Model. *Jurnal Ipteks Terapan, 14*(2), 89–98.

Intelligencer (2017). Extracted from https://nymag.com/intelligencer/2017/02/blackberrys-global-market-share-is-now-0-0.html on 23.01.2021.

Intuit, Great Place to Work. (2019). Extracted from https://www.greatplacetowork.in/great/rated/100-best/Intuit-India#:~:text=Career%20Comeback,comeback%20from%20a%20career%20break.&text=The%20program%20is%20for%20six,into%20full%2Dtime%20employee%20roles

Inyang, B. J. (2010). Strategic human resource management (SHRM): A paradigm shift for achieving sustained competitive advantage in organization. *International Bulletin of Business Administration, 7*(23), 215–243.

Irawanto, D. W. (2015). Employee participation in decision making: Evidence from state owned enterprise in Indonesia. *Management: Journal of contemporary management issues, 20*(1), 159–172.

Itami, H. (1987). *Mobilizing Invisible Assets.* Boston MA: Harvard University Press.

Ivancevich, J. M. (2007). *Human Resource Management.* New York: McGraw-Hill/Irwin.

Jackall, R. (1988). *Moral Mazes: The World of Corporate Managers.* Oxford: Oxford University Press.

Jacobs, R. L. (2002). Institutionalizing organizational change through cascade training. *Journal of European Industrial Training, 26*(2/3/4), 177–182.

Jacobsen, C. B., & Salomonsen, H. H. (2020). Leadership strategies and internal communication in public organizations. *International Journal of Public Sector Management, 34*(2), 137–154.

Jamrog, J. J., & Overholt, M. H. (2004). Building a strategic HR function: Continuing the evolution. *Human Resource Planning, 27*(1), 51–62.

Jeong, I., & Shin, S. J. (2019). High-performance work practices and organizational creativity during organizational change: A collective learning perspective. *Journal of Management, 45*(3), 909–925.

Jha, J. K., Varkkey, B., Agrawal, P., & Singh, N. (2017). Contribution of HR systems in development of ethical climate at workplace: A case study. *South Asian Journal of Human Resources Management, 4*(1), 106–129.

Jobber, D. (2004). *Principles and Practice of Marketing* (4th Ed.). London: McGraw-Hill International.

Johnson, B. (1991), *Polarity Management.* Amherst, MA: HRD Press.

Johnson, C. E. (2012). *Organizational Ethics: A Practical Approach.* Thousand Oaks, CA: Sage Publication, Inc.

Johnson, H. T., & Kaplan, R. S. (1987). *Relevance Lost: The Rise and Fall of Management Accounting.* Boston, MA: Harvard Business School Press.

Johnson, G., Scholes, K., & Whittington, R. (2008). *Exploring corporate strategy: Text & cases.* Harlow: Pearson Education.

Joseph, C. (2013). *Factors That May Cause Change in an Organization.*

Joseph, R., & Reigeluth, C. (2010). The systemic change process in education: A conceptual framework. *Contemporary Educational Technology, 1*(2), 97–117.

Judson, A. (1991). *Changing Behavior in Organizations.* Cambridge, MA: Blackwell Publishing.

Kane, B., & Palmer, I. (1995). Strategic HRM or managing the employment relationship?. *International Journal of Manpower, 16*(5/6), 6–21.

Kang, S. P., Chen, Y., Svihla, V., Gallup, A., Ferris, K., & Datye, A. K. (2020). Guiding change in higher education: An emergent, iterative application of Kotter's change model. *Studies in Higher Education, 1*–20. https://doi.org/10.1080/03075079.2020.1741540

Kanter, R.M. (1985). Managing the human side of change. *Management Review, 74*(4), 52–56.

Kanter, R. M., Stein, B. A., & Jick, T. D. (1992). *The Challenge of Organizational Change*. New York: Free Press.

Kaplan, R.S., & Norton, D.P. (1992). The balanced scorecard–measures that drive performance. *Harvard Business Review, 70*(1), 71–79.

Kaplan, R. S., & Norton, D. P. (1996). *The Balanced Scorecard: Translating Strategy into Action*. Boston, MA: Harvard Business School Press.

Kaplan, R. S., & Norton, D. P. (2004). *Strategy Maps: Converting Intangible Assets into Tangible Outcomes*. Boston, MA: Harvard Business School Press.

Kasemsap, K. (2015). The roles of organizational change management and resistance to change. In A. Goksoy (Ed.), *Organizational Change Management Strategies in Modern Business*. Bulgaria: IGI Global.

Keegan, D. P., Eiler, R. G., & Jones, C. R. (1989). Are your performance measures obsolete?. *Management Accounting, 70*(12), 45–50.

Ketchen Jr, D. J. (2003). Introduction: Raymond E. Miles and Charles C. Snow's organizational strategy, structure, and process. *Academy of Management Perspectives, 17*(4), 95–96.

Kezar, A. (2011). *Understanding and Facilitating Organizational Change in the 21st Century: Recent Research and Conceptualizations: ASHE-ERIC Higher Education Report, Volume 28, Number 4 (Vol. 155)*. Hoboken, NJ: John Wiley & Sons.

Khanna, T., & Raina, A. (2010). TeamLease: Putting India to Work (II) Legally.

Kilcourse, T. (1994). A human resource philosophy. *Management Decision, 32*(9), 37–42.

Kilmann, R, Saxton, M., & Serpa, R. (1985). *Gaining Control of the Corporate Culture*. San Francisco, CA: Jossey Bass.

Kim, A., Han, K., & Kim, Y. (2017). The relationships among participatory management practices for improving firm profitability: Evidence from the South Korean manufacturing industry. *The International Journal of Human Resource Management, 28*(12), 1712–1738.

Kimberly, J. R., & Quinn, R. E. (1984). *The challenge of transition management. Managing organizational transitions*. Homewood, IL: Richard D. Irwin Inc.

King, R.K. (2004). Enhancing SWOT analysis using triz and the bipolar conflict graph: a case study on the Microsoft Corporation. *Proceedings of TRIZCON2004, 6th Annual Altshuller Institute*, April 25-27, Seattle, WA.

Kingston, C., & Caballero, G. (2009). Comparing theories of institutional change. *Journal of Institutional Economics, 5*(2), 151–180.

Kirkman, B. L., Lowe, K. B., & Yaung, D. P. (1999). The challenge of leadership in high performance work organizations. *Journal of Leadership Studies, 5*(2), 3–15.

Klidas, A., Van Den Berg, P. T., & Wilderom, C. P. (2007). Managing employee empowerment in luxury hotels in Europe. *International Journal of Service Industry Management, 18*(1), 70–88.

Kotler, P., & Armstrong, G. (2004). *Principles of Marketing.* Upper Saddle River, NJ: Prentice Hall.

Kotter, J. (1995). Leading change - Why transformation efforts fail. *Harvard Business Review*, *86*, 97–103.

Kotter, J. P. (1996). *Leading Change*. Boston, MA: Harvard Business School Press.

Kotter, J. P., & Schlesinger, L. A. (1979). Choosing strategies for change. *Harvard Business Review*, *57*(2), 106–114.

Kozlowski, S. W. J., Gully, S. M., Nason, E. R., & Smith, E. M. (1999). Developing adaptive teams: A theory of compilation and performance across levels and time. In D. R. Ilgen & E. D. Pulakos (Eds.), *The Changing Nature of Performance: Implications for Staffing, Motivation, And Development* (pp. 240–292). San Francisco, CA: Jossey-Bass Inc. Publishers.

Kritsonis, A. (2005). Comparison of Change Theories. *International Journal of Management, Business, and Administration*, *8*(1), 1–7.

Kryscynski, D., Reeves, C., Stice-Lusvardi, R., Ulrich, M., & Russell, G. (2018). Analytical abilities and the performance of HR professionals. *Human Resource Management*, *57*(3), 715–738.

Kuo, Y. L., & Chen, I. J. (2019). Facilitating a change model in age-friendly hospital certification: Strategies and effects. *PloS one, 14*(4), e0213496.

Kurti, E., & Haftor, D. (2015, September). Barriers and enablers of digital business model transformation. European *Conference on Information Management and Evaluation (p. 262)*. Academic Conferences International Limited.

Kwon Choi, B., Koo Moon, H., & Ko, W. (2013). An organization's ethical climate, innovation, and performance: Effects of support for innovation and performance evaluation. *Management Decision*, *51*(6), 1250–1275.

Kyle, N. (1993). Staying with the flow of change. *Journal for Quality and Participation*, *16*(4), 34–42.

Lambert, D. E. (2019). Addressing challenges to homeland security information sharing in American policing: Using Kotter's leading change model. *Criminal Justice Policy Review*, *30*(8), 1250–1278.

Lander, M. W., & Heugens, P. P. (2017). Better together: Using meta-analysis to explore complementarities between ecological and institutional theories of organization. *Organization Studies*, *38*(11), 1573–1601.

Langlois, R. N. (1992). Transaction-cost economics in real time. *Industrial and corporate change*, *1*(1), 99–127.

Langlois, R. N., & Robertson, P. L. (1995). *Firms, Markets and Economic Change*. London: Routledge.

Lartey, F. M. (2020). Chaos, complexity, and contingency theories: A comparative analysis and application to the 21st century organization. *Journal of Business Administration Research*, *9*(1), 44–51.

Latta, G. F. (2020). A complexity analysis of organizational culture, leadership and engagement: integration, differentiation and fragmentation. *International Journal of Leadership in Education*, *23*(3), 274–299.

Lau, C. M., & Woodman, R. W. (1995). Understanding organizational change: A schematic perspective. *Academy of Management Journal, 38*(2), 537–554.

Laursen, K. (2002). The importance of sectoral differences in the application of complementary HRM practices for innovation performance. *International Journal of the Economics of Business, 9*(1), 139–156.

Lave, J. (1988). *Cognition in Practice*. Cambridge, UK: Cambridge University Press.

Lawler III, E. E. (1986). *High-Involvement Management. Participative Strategies for Improving Organizational Performance*. San Francisco, CA: Jossey-Bass Inc., Publishers.

Lawler III, E. E., Levenson, A. R., & Boudreau, J. W. (2004). HR metrics and analytics: Use and impact. *People and Strategy, 27*(4), 27.

Lawson, S. (2016). 3D Robotics means business with its new enterprise drone system. *PCWorld*. Extracted from https://www.pcworld.com/article/3041 632/internet-of-things/3d-robotics-means-business-with-its-new-enterprise-drone-system.html on 23.01.2021.

Leavitt, H. J., & Whistler, T. L. (1958). Management in the 1980s. *Harvard Business Review, 36*, 41–48.

Ledford, G. E., & Lawler, E. E. (1994). Research on employee participation: Beating a dead horse?. *Academy of Management Review, 19*(4), 633–636.

Lengnick-Hall, C. A., & Lengnick-Hall, M. L. (1988). Strategic human re-source management: A review of the literature and a proposed typology. *Academy of Management Review, 13*(3), 454–470.

Leung, K., Bhagat, R., Buchan, N. R., Erez, M., & Gibson, C. B. (2005). Culture and international business: Recent advances and their implications for future research. *Journal of International Business Studies, 36*(4), 357–378.

Levitan, S. A., & Werneke, D. (1984). *Productivity--problems, prospects, and policies (No. 40)*. Johns Hopkins University Press.

Levitt, B., & March, J. G. (1988). Organizational learning. *Annual Review of Sociology, 14*(1), 319–338.

Levy, A. (1986). Second-order planned change: Definition and con-ceptualization. *Organizational Dynamics, 15*(1), 5–23.

Lewin, K. (1947). Frontiers in group dynamics. In D. Cartwright (Ed.), *Field Theory in Social Science*. London: Social Science Paperbacks.

Lewin, K. (1951). *Field Theory in Social Science*. New York, NY: Harper & Row.

Lewin, K., Lippitt, R., & White, R. K. (1939). Patterns of aggressive beha-viour in experimentally created "social climates". *Journal of Social Psychology, 10*(2), 269–299.

Lientz, B. P., & Rea, K. P. (2004). *Breakthrough IT Change Management: How to Get Enduring Change Results*. Amsterdam: Routledge.

Likert, R. (1961). *New Patterns of Management*. New York: McGraw-Hill.

Likert, R. (1967). *The Human Organization: Its Management and Value*. New York: McGray-Hill.

Lines, R. (2007). Using power to install strategy: the relationships between expert power, position power, influence tactics and implementation success. *Journal of Change Management*, *7*(2), 143–170.

Liu, H., Zhang, X., Chang, R., & Wang, W. (2017). A research regarding the relationship among intensive care nurses' self-esteem, job satisfaction and subjective well-being. *International Journal of Nursing Sciences*, *4*(3), 291–295.

Lloyd, C., & Rawlinson, M. (1992). New technology and human resource management. In P. Blyton & P. Turnbull (Eds.), *Reassessing Human Resource Management* (pp. 185–199). London: Sage Publications.

Lloyd, C. B., & Duffy, N. (1995). Families in transition. In J. Bruce, C. B. Lloyd & A. Leonard, (Eds.), *Families in Focus: New Perspectives on Mothers. Fathers, and Children* (pp. 5–23). New York: The Population Council.

Lok, P., & Crawford, J. (2000). The application of a diagnostic model and surveys in organizational development. *Journal of Managerial Psychology*, *15*(2), 108–124.

Lopes, L. L. (1994). Psychology and economics: Perspectives on risk, co-operation, and the marketplace. *Advances in Psychology*, *45*(1), 197–227.

Lorange, P., & Murphy, D. (1984). Bringing Human Resource Strategy into Strategic Planning: Systems Designs Considerations. In C. Fombrun, N. M. Tichy & M. A. Devanna (Eds.), *Strategic Human Resource Management*. New York: John Wiley & Sons.

Lorsch, J. (1985). Strategic myopia: Culture as an invisible barrier to change. In R. H. Kilmann, M. J. Saxton & R. Serpa (Eds.), *Gaining Control of the Corporate Culture*. San Francisco, CA: Jossey Bass.

Lowe, K. B., Kroeck, K. G., & Sivasubramaniam, N. (1996). Effectiveness correlates of transformational and transactional leadership: A meta-analytic review of the MLQ literature. *Leadership Quarterly*, *7*(3), 385–425.

Luecke, R. (2003). *Managing Change and Transition*. Boston, MA: Harvard Business School Press.

Lundberg, C. C. (1984). Strategies for Organisational Transitioning. In J. R. Kimberly & R. E. Quinn (Eds.), *Managing Organizational Transitions* (pp. 60–82). Homewood, IL: Irwin.

Luthans, K. W., & Sommer, S. M. (2005). Impact of high performance work on industry-level outcomes. *Journal of Managerial Issues*, *17*(3), 327–345.

Lynch, R. L., & Cross, K. F. (1991). Measure up-the essential guide to measuring. *Business Performance*. London: Mandarin.

Mabey, C., & Salaman, G. (1995). *Strategic Human Resource Management*. Great Britain: Blackwell.

MacDuffie, J. P. (1995). Human resource bundles and manufacturing performance: Organizational logic and flexible production systems in the world auto industry. *Industrial and Labor Relations Review*, *48*(2), 197–221.

Mahoney, J., & Thelen, K. (2010). *Explaining institutional change: Ambiguity, agency, and power*. Cambridge, UK: Cambridge University Press.

Maier, R., & Remus, U. (2002). Defining process-oriented knowledge management strategies. *Knowledge and Process Management, 9*(2), 103–118.

Mahindra, Great Place to Work (2019). Extracted from https://www.greatplacetowork.in/great/rated/100-best/Mahindra-and-Mahindra-Automotive-and-Farm-Equipment-Sectors on 08.01.2021.

Malone, T. W. (1994). Commentary on Suchman article and Winograd response. *Computer supported cooperative work (CSCW), 3*(1), 37–38.

Mannan, M. A. (1987). *Workers' Participation in Managerial Decision-making: A Study in a Developing Country*. New Delhi: Daya Publishing House.

Manyika, J., Chui, M., Brown, B., Bughin, J., Dobbs, R., Roxburgh, C., & Byers, A. (2011). *Big Data: The Next Frontier for Innovation, Competition and Productivity*. McKinsey & Company.

March, J. G. (1981). Footnotes to organizational change. *Administrative Science Quarterly, 26*, 563–577.

March, J. G., & Simon, H.A. (1958). *Organisations*. New York: Wiley.

Marhraoui, M. A., & El Manouar, A. (2020). Organizational agility and the complementary enabling role of IT and human resources: Proposition of a new framework. In *ICT for an Inclusive World* (pp. 55–65). Cham: Springer.

Marks, M. L. (2007). A framework for facilitating adaptation to organizational transition. *Journal of Organizational Change Management, 20*(5), 721–739.

Marr, B. (2015). 3 Ways The Internet of Things Will Change Every Business. *Forbes*. Extracted from https://www.forbes.com/sites/bernardmarr/2015/08/17/3-ways-the-internet-of-things-will-change-every-business/#6dc7256d1981 on 23.01.2021.

Marschke, E., Preziosi, R., & Harrington, W. J. (2009). Professionals and executives support a relationship between organizational commitment and spirituality in the workplace. *Journal of Business & Economics Research, 7*(8), 33–48.

Marschke, E., Preziosi, R., & Harrington, W. J. (2011). How sales personnel view the relationship between job satisfaction and spirituality in the workplace. *Journal of Organizational Culture, Communication and Conflict, 15*(2), 71–109.

Martell, K., & Carroll, S. J. (1995). How strategic is HRM?. *Human Resource Management, 34*(2), 253–267.

Martin, J., & Siehl, C. (1983). Organisational culture and counter culture: An uneasy symbiosis. *Organizational Dynamics, 12*(2), 52–64.

Martin, A. J., Jones, E. S., & Callan, V. J. (2005). The role of psychological climate in facilitating employee adjustment during organizational change. *European Journal of Work and Organizational Psychology, 14*(3), 263–289.

McCrae, R. R., & Costa, P. T., Jr. (1986). Personality, coping, and coping effectiveness in an adult sample. *Journal of Personality, 54*(2), 385–405.

McDonald, T., & Siegall, M. (1992). The effects of technological self-efficacy and job focus on job performance, attitudes, and withdrawal behaviors. *Journal of Psychology, 126*(5), 465–475.

McLaughlin, C. (1998). Spirituality at work. *The Bridging Tree, 1*(11).

McLellan, C. (2015). *Artificial Intelligence In Business: The State Of Play And Future Prospects.* ZDNET. (2015, September 1). Web. 27 Mar. 2017.

Meier, S. S., & Melar, C. (2014). Integrating informal learning into corporate learning via social media. In Jelena J. & Raymond C. (Eds.), *Technological and Social Environments for Interactive Learning.* Santa Rosa, CA: Informing Science Press.

Mello, J. A. (2006). *Strategic Human Resource Management* (2nd ed.). Mason, OH: Thompson, South-Western.

Merton, R. (1940). Bureaucratic structure and personality. *Social Forces, 18,* 560–568.

Meyer, A. D., Goes, J. B. (1988). Organizational assimilation of innovations: A multilevel contextual analysis. *Academy of Management Journal, 31*(4), 897–923.

Meyer, A. D., Goes, J. D., & Brooks, G. R. (1993). Organizations reacting to hyper turbulence. In G. P. Huber & W.H. Glick (eds.), *Organizational Change and Redesign* (pp. 66–111). New York: Oxford University Press.

Mierke, J. & Williamson, V. (2017). A framework for achieving organizational culture change. Extracted from https://harvest.usask.ca/handle/10388/7735 on 04.01.2021

Miles, R. E., & Snow, C. C. (1984). Fit, failure, and the hall of fame. *California Management Review, 26*(3), 10–28.

Miller, K. I., & Monge, P. R. (1986). Participation, satisfaction, and productivity: A meta-analytic review. *Academy of Management Journal, 29*(4), 727–753.

Miller, A. R., & Yeager, R. J. (1993). Managing change: A corporate application of rational-emotive therapy. *Journal of Rational-emotive and Cognitive-behavior Therapy, 11*(2), 65–76.

Milliman, J., Czaplewski, A. J., & Ferguson, J. (2003). Workplace spirituality and employee work attitudes: An exploratory empirical assessment. *Journal of Organizational Change Management, 16*(4), 426–447.

Mintzberg, H. (1987). *Crafting Strategy.* Boston, MA: Harvard Business Review.

Mischel, L. J., & Northcraft, G. B. (1997). "I think we can, I think we can..." The role of efficacy beliefs in group and team effectiveness. In B. Markovsky (Eds.), *Advances in group processes* (pp. 177 – 197). Greenwich, CT: JAI Press.

Mishra, P., Shukla, B., & Sujatha, R. (2017). Changing contours of performance management paradigm. *International Journal of Applied Business and Economic Research, 15*(17), 353–371.

Mishra, P., Shukla, B., & Sujatha, R. (2019). Vision actualisation and spirituality: A theoretical model. *Purushartha, 11*(02), 14–24.

Mitchell, T. R. (1973). Motivation and participation: An integration. *Academy of Management Journal, 16*(4), 670 – 679.

Mitroff, I. I., & Denton, E. A. (1999). A study of spirituality in the workplace. *Sloan Management Review, 40*(4), 83–92.

Mohrman, A. (1989). *Large-scale Organization Change.* San Francisco: Jossey-Bass.

Mondore, S., Douthitt, S., & Carson, M. (2011). Maximizing the impact and effectiveness of HR analytics to drive business outcomes. *People and Strategy, 34*(2), 2.

Moran, J. W., & Brightman, B. K. (2001). Leading organizational change. *Career Development International, 6*(2), 111–118.

Morgan, G. (1986). *Images of Organization.* Thousand Oaks, CA: Sage.

Morrison, E. W. (1996). Organizational citizenship behavior as a critical link between HRM practices and service quality. *Human Resource Management, 35*(4), 493–512.

Mortensen, M., Doherty, N. F., & Robinson, S. (2015). Operational research from Taylorism to Terabytes: A research agenda for the analytics age. *European Journal of Operational Research, 241*(3), 583–595.

Motowidlo, S. J., & Van Scotter, J. R. (1994). Evidence that task performance should be distinguished from contextual performance. *Journal of Applied psychology, 79*(4), 475–480.

Moxley, R. S. (1999). *Leadership and Spirit: Breathing New Vitality and Energy into Individuals and Organizations.* San Francisco, CA: Jossey-Bass Publishers.

Mumford, E. (1972). *Job Satisfaction – a Study of Computer Specialists.* London: Longmans.

Murphy, P. (1989). Creating ethical corporate structures. *Sloan Management Review, 30*(2), 81–87.

Murphy, K., Torres, E., Ingram, W., & Hutchinson, J. (2018). A review of high performance work practices (HPWPs) literature and recommendations for future research in the hospitality industry. *International Journal of Contemporary Hospitality Management, 30*(1), 365–388.

Myers, K., & Robbins, M. (1991). 10 rules for change. *Executive Excellence, 8*(5), 9–10.

Myspace. (2019). Extracted from https://en.wikipedia.org/wiki/Myspace on 07.05.2019.

Nadler, D. (1981). Managing organizational change: An integrative perspective. *The Journal of Applied Behavioural Science, 17*(2),191–211.

Nadler, D. (1988). Organizational frame-bending: Types of change in the complex organization. In R. Kilmann & T. Covin (eds.), *Corporate Transformation* (pp. 66–83). San Francisco, CA: Jossey-Bass.

Nadler, D., & Tushman, M. (1995). Types of organizational change: from incremental improvement to discontinuous transformation. In D. A. Nadler (Eds.), *Discontinuous Change: Leading Organizational Transformation* (pp. 15–34). San Francisco, CA: Jossey-Bass.

Nadler, D. A., Tushman, M., & Hatvany, N. G. (1980). A model for diagnosing organisational behaviour: Applying a congruence perspective. *Organizational Dynamics, 9*(2), 35–51.

Nag, R., Hambrick, D. C., & Chen, M. J. (2007). What is strategic management, really? Inductive derivation of a consensus definition of the field. *Strategic Management Journal, 28*(9), 935–955.

Nason, R. S., & Wiklund, J. (2018). An assessment of resource-based theorizing on firm growth and suggestions for the future. *Journal of Management, 44*(1), 32–60.

Neal, J. A., & Tromley, C. L. (1995). From incremental change to retrofit: creating high-performance work systems. *The Academy of Management Executive, 9*(1), 42–53.

Neck, C. P., & Milliman, J. F. (1994). Thought self-leadership: Finding spiritual fulfillment in organizational life. *Journal of Managerial Psychology, 9*(6), 9–16.

Neely, A. D., Gregory, M. J., & Platts, K. W. (1995). Performance measurement system design: A literature review and research agenda. *International Journal of Operations and Production Management, 15*(4), 80–116.

Nel, P. S., Werner, A., Poisat, P., Sono, T., Du Plessis, A. J., & Nqalo, O. (2011). *Human Resources Management* (8th ed.). South Africa: Oxford University Press.

Nelissen, P., & van Selm, M.(2008). Surviving organizational change: How management communication helps balance mixed feelings. *Corporate Communications: An International Journal, 13*(3), 306–318.

Nelson, R. R., & Winter, S. G. (1982). *An Evolutionary Theory of Economic Change.* Cambridge, MA: Harvard University Press.

Nelson, A., Cooper, C. L., & Jackson, P. R. (1995). Uncertainty amidst change: The impact of privatization on employee job satisfaction and well-being. *Journal of Occupational and Organizational Psychology, 68*(1), 57–71.

Neubauer, R., Tarling, A., & Wade, M. (2017). Redefining leadership for a digital age. Global Centre for Digital Business Transformation and metaBeratung GmbH, 1–15. Retrieved from https://www.imd.org/globalassets/dbt/docs/redefining-leadership

Nicholson, N. (1984). Organisational culture, ideology and management. In J. Hunt, D. Hosking, C. Schriesheim & R. Stewart (Eds.), *Leaders and Managers.* New York: Pergamon Press.

Nicholson, N., Rees, A., & Brooks-Rooney, A. (1990). Strategy, innovation, and performance. *Journal of Management Studies, 27,* 511–534.

Noe, R. A., Hollenbeck, J. R., Gerhart, B., & Wright, P. M. (2000). *Human Resources Management: Gaining Competitive Advantage* (3rd ed.). Boston, MA: McGraw-Hill Higher Education.

Nordström, K. A., & Ridderstrále, J. (2002). *Funky Business. Talent makes Capital Dance.* Pearson Education.

Nørreklit, H., Kure, N., & Trenca, M. (2018). Balanced Scorecard. *The International Encyclopedia of Strategic Communication,* 1–6.

Novac, Great Place to Work, (2020). Extracted from https://www.greatplacetowork.in/great/profile/india-best/Novac-Technology-Solutions on 08.01.2021.

NTPC Internal Communications. (2019). Extracted from https://www.india-tvnews.com/technology/apps-ntpc-samvaad-app-an-example-for-other-organisations-570285 on 08.01.2021

Nyhan, R. C. (2000). Changing the paradigm: Trust and its role in public sector organizations. *The American Review of Public Administration, 30*(1), 87–109.

O'Connor, C. A. (1993). Resistance: The repercussions of change. *Leadership & Organization Development Journal, 14*(6), 30–36.

Ocasio, W., & Joseph, J. (2018). The attention-based view of great strategies. *Strategy Science, 3*(1), 289–294.

Odendaal, A., Robbins, S. P., & Roodt, G. (2004). *Organisational Behaviour: Global and Southern African Perspectives*. Cape Town: Pearson Limited.

Odor, H. O. (2018). Organisational change and development. *European Journal of Business Management, 10*(7), 58–66.

Okumus, F., & Hemmington, N. (1998). Barriers and resistance to change in hotel firms: An investigation at unit level. *International Journal of Contemporary Hospitality Management, 10*(7), 283–288.

Olve, N., Roy, J., & Wetter, M. (1999). *Performance Drivers: a Practical Guide to Using the Balanced Scorecard*. Chichester: John Wiley and Sons.

Omer, S. K. (2019). SWOT analysis implementation's significance on strategy planning Samsung mobile company as an example. *Journal of Process Management. New Technologies, 7*(1), 56–62.

Oreg, S. (2006). Personality, context and resistance to organizational change. *European Journal of Work and Organizational Psychology, 15*(1), 73–101.

Orlitzky, M., & Frenkel, S. J. (2005). Alternative Pathways to High Performance Workplaces. *International Journal of Human Resource Management, 16*(8), 1325–1348.

Ostrom, E. (2005). *Understanding institutional diversity*. Princeton, NJ: Princeton University Press.

Oswick, C., & Grant, D. (2016). Re-imagining images of organization: A conversation with Gareth Morgan. *Journal of Management Inquiry, 25*(3), 338–343.

Ottaway, R. (1976). A change strategy to implement new norms, new styles and new environment in the work organisation. *Personnel Review, 5*(1), 13–18.

Palmer, I. (2005). *Managing Organisational Change*. New Delhi: McGraw-Hill Education (India) Pvt Limited.

Pande, S., & Basak, S. (2012). *Human Resource Management: Text and Cases*. New Delhi: Pearson Education.

Pareek, U., & Rao, T. V. (1999). *Designing and Managing Human Resource Systems*. New Delhi: Oxford University Press and IBH.

Pascale, R. (1985). The paradox of "corporate culture": Reconciling ourselves to socialization. *California Management Review, 27*(2), 26–41.

Pathak, H. (2011). *Organizational Change*. New Delhi: Pearson Education India.

Paton, R. A., & McCalman, J. (2000). *Change Management: A Guide to Effective Implementation* (2nd ed.). London: SAGE Publications.

Pattanayak, B. (2009). *Human Resource Management*. New Delhi: PHI Learning Private Limited.

Patterson, K. (2002). *Crucial Conversations: Tools for Talking When Stakes are High*. New York: Tata McGraw-Hill Education.

Pennings, J. M. (1985). *Organisational Strategy and Change*. San Francisco, CA: Jossey-Bass.

Penrose, E. T. (1959). *The Theory of the Growth of the Firm*. Oxford: Basil Blackwell.

Smith, M. R., & Marx, L. (eds.). (1984). *Does Technology Drive History? The Dilemma of Technological Determinism*. Cambridge, MA: MIT Press.

Perry, M. J. (2017). Fortune 500 firms 1955 v. 2017. Extracted from http://www.aei.org/publication/fortune-500-firms-1955-v-2017-only-12-remain-thanks-to-the-creative-destruction-that-fuels-economic-prosperity/ on 23.01.2021.

Peters, T., & Waterman, R. (1982). *In Search of Excellence: Lessons from American's Best-Run Companies*. New York: Harper & Row.

Petersen, L. B., Person, R., & Nash, C. (2014). *Connect: How to Use Data and Experience Marketing to Create Lifetime Customers*. Hoboken: John Wiley & Sons.

Pettigrew, A. M. (1985). *The Awakening Giant*. Oxford, UK: Blackwell Publishers.

Pfeffer, J. (1994). *Competitive advantage through people*. Boston, MA: Harvard Business School Press.

Pfeffer, J., & Veiga, J. F. (1999). Putting people first for organisational success. *Academy of Management Executive, 13*(2), 37–48

Pfeifer, T., Schmitt, R., & Voigt, T. (2005). Managing change: Quality-oriented design of strategic change processes. *The TQM Magazine, 17*(4), 297–308.

Piderit, S. K. (2000). Rethinking resistance and recognizing ambivalence: A multidimensional view of attitudes toward an organizational change. *Academy of Management Review, 25*(4), 783–794.

Pierce, J. L., & Delbecq, A. L. (1977). Organization structure, individual attitudes and innovation. *Academy of Management Review, 2*(1), 27–37.

Pietersen, W. (2002). The Mark Twain dilemma: The theory and practice of change leadership. *The Journal of Business Strategy, 23*(5), 32–37.

Podsakoff, P. M., Ahearne, M., & MacKenzie, S. B. (1997). Organizational citizenship behavior and the quantity and quality of work group performance. *Journal of Applied Psychology, 82*(2), 262–270.

Porter, M. E. (1980). *Competitive Strategy*. New York: Free Press.

Porter, M. E. (1985). *The Competitive Advantage: Creating and Sustaining Superior Performance*. New York: Harvard Business Press.

Porter, M. E. (1998). What is strategy?. In S. Segal-Horn (Eds.), *The Strategy Reader* (pp. 17–99). Malden, MA: Blackwell Publishing.

Posadzińska, I., Słupska, U., & Karaszewski, R. (2020). The attitudes and actions of the superior and the participative management style. *European Research Studies, 23*, 488–501.

Power, B. (2015). Artificial intelligence is almost ready for business. *Harvard Business Review.*

Prahalad, C. K., & Hamel, G. (1990). The core competence of the corporation. *Harvard Business Review, 68*(3),79–91.

Prasad, L. M. (2006). *Human Resource Management* (475–493). Delhi: Sultan Chand & Sons.

Proctor, R. A. (1992). Structured and creative approaches to strategy formulation. *Management Research News, 15*(1), 13–19.

Radulescu, C. V., & Ioan, I. (2009). Economical crisis and the European Union's cohesion policy. *Management Research and Practice, 1*(1),62–67.

Raeder, S. (2019). The role of human resource management practices in managing organizational change. *Gruppe. Interaktion. Organisation. Zeitschrift für Angewandte Organisationspsychologie (GIO), 50*(2), 169–191.

Reed, R., & DeFillippi, R. J. (1990). Causal ambiguity, barriers to imitation, and sustainable competitive advantage. *Academy of management review, 15*(1), 88–102.

Reed, M., & Anthony, P. (1992). Professionalizing management and managing professionalization: British management in the 1980s. *Journal of Management Studies, 29*(5), 591–613.

Reichers, A. E., Wanous, J. P., & Austin, J. T. (1997). Understanding and managing cynicism about organizational change. *Academy of Management Executive, 11*(1), 48–59.

Rennie, W. H. (2003). *The role of human resource management and the human resource professional in the new economy.* (Doctoral dissertation, University of Pretoria).

Rice, R. E., & Rogers, E. M. (1980). Reinvention in the innovation process. *Knowledge, 1*(4), 499–514.

Riggs, M. L., Warka, J., Babasa, B., Betancourt, R., & Hooker, S. (1994). Development and validation of self-efficacy and outcome expectancy scales for job-related applications. *Educational and psychological measurement, 54*(3), 793–802.

Rimanoczy, I., & Pearson, T. (2010). Role of HR in the new world of sustainability. *Industrial and Commercial Training, 42*(1), 11–17.

Romanelli, E., & Tushman, M. L. (1994). Organizational transformation as punctuated equilibrium: An empirical test. *Academy of Management Journal, 37*(5), 1141–1166.

Rooney, P. M. (1988). Worker participation in employee-owned firms. *Journal of Economic Issues, 22* (2), 451–458.

Roscoe, S., Subramanian, N., Jabbour, C. J., & Chong, T. (2019). Green human resource management and the enablers of green organisational culture: Enhancing a firm's environmental performance for sustainable development. *Business Strategy and the Environment, 28*(5), 737–749.

Rosenzweig, P. M., & Nohria, N. (1994). Influences on human resource management practices in multinational corporations. *Journal of International Business Studies, 25*(2), 229–251.

Rosman, M. Y., Shah, F. A., Hussain, J., & Hussain, A. (2013). Factors affecting the role of human resource department in private healthcare sector in Pakistan: A case study of Rehman Medical Institute (RMI). *Research Journal of Recent Studies, 2*(1), 84–90.

Rothwell, W. J. (2013). *Performance consulting: applying performance improvement in human resource development.* Hoboken, NJ: John Wiley & Sons.

Rotter, J. B. (1966). Generalized expectancies for internal versus external control of reinforcement. *Psychological monographs: General and applied, 80*(1), 1.

Rumelt, R. P. (1991). How much does industry matter?. *Strategic Management Journal, 12*(3), 167–185.

Rush, M. C., Schoel, W. A., & Barnard, S. M. (1995). Psychological resiliency in the public sector:" Hardiness" and pressure for change. *Journal of Vocational Behavior, 46*(1), 17–39.

Sabri, E. H., Gupta, A. P., & Beitler, M. A. (2006). *Purchase Order Management Best Practices: Process, Technology, and Change Management.* New York: J. Ross Publishing.

Sadler, T. (1995). *HRM: Developing a strategic approach.* London: Kogan Page.

Sagie, A., Elizur, D., & Greenbaum, C. W. (1985). Job experience, persuasion strategy and resistance to change: An experimental study. *Journal of Organizational Behavior, 6*(2), 157–162.

Salem, P., & Williams, M. L. (1984). Uncertainty and satisfaction: The importance of information in hospital communication. *Journal of Applied Communication Research, 12*(2), 75–89.

Sarayreh, B. H., Khudair, H., & Barakat, E. A. (2013). Comparative study: The Kurt Lewin of change management. *International Journal of Computer and Information Technology, 2*(4), 626–629.

Schein, E. H. (1967). Organizational socialization and the profession of management. *Sloan Management Review, 30*(1), 53–65.

Schein, E. H. (1984). Coming to a new awareness of organizational culture. *Sloan Management Review, 25*(2), 3–16.

Schein, E. H. (1985). *Organizational Culture and Leadership.* San Francisco, CA: Jossey-Bass.

Schein, E. H. (1996). Kurt Lewin's change theory in the field and in the classroom: Notes toward a model of managed learning. *Systems Practice, 9*(1), 27–47.

Schuler, R. S., & Jackson, S. E. (1987). Linking competitive strategies with human resource management practices. *The Academy of Management Executive, 1*(3), 207–219.

Scott, C. D., & Jaffe, D. T. (1988). Survive and thrive in times of change. *Training & Development Journal, 42*(4), 25–28.

Selznick, P. (2011). *Leadership in Administration: A Sociological Interpretation*. New Orleans, LA: Quid Pro Books.

Senge, P. M. (1990). *The Fifth Discipline: The Art & Practice of the Learning Organization*. New York: Currency Doubleday.

Senge, P. M., & Kaeufer, K. H. (2000). Creating change. *Executive Excellence, 17*(10), 4-4.

Senge, P., Kleiner, A., Roberts, C., Ross, R., Roth, G., Smith, B., & Guman, E. C. (1999). The dance of change: The challenges to sustaining momentum in learning organizations. *Performance Improvement, 38*(5), 55–58.

Senior, B. (2002). *Organisational Change* (2nd ed.). London: Prentice Hall.

Shankarnarayanan, S. (2000). ERP systems—using IT to gain a competitive advantage. Expressindia Co.

Shapiro, D. L., Lewicki, R. J., & Devine, P. (1995). When do employees choose deceptive tactics to stop unwanted organizational change?: A relational perspective. *Research on negotiation in organizations, 5*, 155–184.

Shenkar, O., & Zeira, Y. (1987). Human resources management in international joint ventures: Directions for research. *Academy of Management Review, 12*(3), 546–557.

Shimoni, B. (2017). What is resistance to change? A habitus-oriented approach. *Academy of Management Perspectives, 31*(4), 257–270.

Shivani, S., Mukherjee, S. K., & Sharan, R. (2006). Socio-cultural influences on Indian entrepreneurs: The need for appropriate structural interventions. *Journal of Asian Economics, 17*(1), 5–13.

Shukla, B., & Rizvi, Y. (2009). Managing organisation change: An empirical study of human resource interventions in mergers and acquisitions. *International Journal of Knowledge, Culture and Change Management, 9*(7), 27–52.

Simms, H. (2005). *Organisational Behaviour and Change Management*. Cambridge: Select Knowledge Limited.

Sinclair, A. (1993). Approaches to organisational culture and ethics. *Journal of Business Ethics, 12*(1), 63–73.

Sirkin, H. L., Keenan, P., & Jackson, A. (2005). The hard side of change management. *Harvard Business Review, 83*(10), 109–118.

Skoog, M. (2020). Towards a more sustainable and integrated performance management. *Accounting for Sustainability*, 73–86. https://doi.org/10.4324/9781003037200

Speckbacher, G., Bischof, J., & Pfeiffer, T. (2003). A descriptive analysis on the implementation of balanced scorecards in German-speaking countries. *Management Accounting Research, 14*(4), 361–388.

Spencer, L. M., & Spencer, S. M. (1993). *Competence at Work*. New York: Wiley.

Spencer, S. J., Josephs, R. A., & Steele, C. M. (1993). Low self-esteem: The uphill struggle for self-integrity. In *Self-esteem* (pp. 21–36). New York: Springer.

Spiker, B. K. (1994). Making change stick. *Industry Week/IW, 243*(5), 45-45.

Spiker, B. K., & Lesser, E. (1995). We have met the enemy. *Journal of Business Strategy, 16*(2), 17–21.

Srivastav, S. (2019). Extracted from https://appinventiv.com/blog/uber-statistics/ on 23.01.2021.

Stalk, G., Evans, P., & Shulman, L. (1992). Competing on capabilities: The new rules of corporate strategy. *Harvard Business Review, 70*, 57 – 69.

Stammer, N., & Wilson, S. (2013). *CompTIA Cloud+ Certification Study Guide (Exam CV0-001)*. New York: McGraw Hill Professional.

Stanley Budner, N. Y. (1962). Intolerance of ambiguity as a personality variable. *Journal of Personality, 30*(1), 29–50.

Steele, C. M. (1988). The psychology of self affirmation: Sustaining the integrity of the self. In A. L. Berkowitz (Ed.), *Advances in Experimental Social Psychology (Vol. 12*, pp. 261—302). Sandiego, CA: Academic Press.

Steinburg, C. (1992). Taking charge of change. *Training and Development, 46*(3), 26–32.

Stewart, T. A., & Woods, W. (1996). Taking on the last bureaucracy. *Fortune, 133*(1), 105–107.

Storey, J. (1992). *Developments in the Management of Human Resources.* Oxford: Blackwell Publishers.

Suchman, L. (1987). *Plans and Situated Action.* Cambridge, UK: Cambridge University Press.

Sullivan, M. F., & Guntzelman, J. (1991). The grieving process in cultural change. *The Health Care Supervisor, 10*(2), 28–33.

Syndell, M. A. (2008). *The role of emotional intelligence in transformational leadership Style.* (Doctoral dissertation, Capella University).

Szierbowski-Seibel, K. (2018). Strategic human resource management and its impact on performance–do Chinese organizations adopt appropriate HRM policies?. *Journal of Chinese Human Resource Management.* https://doi.org/10.1108/JCHRM-07-2017-0017

Tamkin, P. (2004). *High performance work practices* (pp. 1–16). Brighton, England: Institute for Employment Studies.

Tata Communication, Great Place to Work. (2019). Extracted from https://www.greatplacetowork.in/great/rated/100-best/Tata-Communications on 08.01.2021.

Teece, D. J. (2018). Dynamic capabilities as (workable) management systems theory. *Journal of Management & Organization, 24*(3), 359–368.

Telematics. (2021). Extracted from http://www.dictionary.com/browse/telematics?s=t on 21.01.2021.

Thornhill, A., Lewis, P., Millmore, M., & Saunders, M. (2000). *Managing change: a human resource strategy approach.* Harlow: Financial Times/Prentice Hall.

Tichy, N. M. (1983). Managing organizational transformations. *Human Resource Management, 22*(1-2), 45–60.

Tiwari, P., & Saxena, K. (2012). Human resource management practices: A comprehensive review. *Pakistan Business Review, 9*(2), 669–705.

Todnem By, R. (2005). Organisational change management: A critical review. *Journal of Change Management, 5*(4), 369–380.

Tomer, J. F. (1987). *Organizational Capital: The Path to Higher Productivity and Well-being.* New York: Praeger publishers.

Torrington, D., & Hall, L. (1995). *Personnel Management: HRM In Action.* Hemel Hempstead: Prentice Hall.

Trevino, L. K., & Nelson, K. A. (2011). *Managing Business Ethics: Straight Talk About How to Do It Right.* Hoboken: John Wiley & Sons, Inc.

Tripathi, P. C. (2006). *Human Resource Development.* Delhi: Sultan Chand & Sons.

Trompenaars, F., & Woolliams, P. (2003). *Business Across Cultures.* Chichester: Capstone.

Trompenaars, F., & Hampden-Turner, C. (2004). *Managing People Across Cultures.* Chichester: Capstone.

Truss, C., & Gratton, L. (1994). Strategic human resource management: A conceptual approach. *Journal of Human Resource Management, 5*(3), 663–686.

Turner, B. (1971). *Exploring the Industrial Subculture.* London: Macmillan.

Turner, J. (1999). Regulars-Control-Ethics-Spirituality in the workplace. *CA Magazine-Chartered Accountant, 132*(10), 41–42.

Turner, S. (2002). *Tools for Success: A Manager's Guide.* London: McGraw-Hill.

Turner, P. (2020). Engagement Driven Strategic HRM. In *Employee Engagement in Contemporary Organizations* (pp. 223–256). Cham: Palgrave Macmillan.

Tushman, M. L., & Romanelli, E. (1985). Organizational evolution: A metamorphosis model of convergence and reorientation. *Research in Organizational Behavior, 7*, 171–222.

Ulrich, D. (1997). *Human resource champions: The next agenda for adding value and delivering results.* Boston, MA: Harvard Business School.

Ulrich, D., & Brockbank, W. (2005). *The HR value proposition.* Boston, MA: Harvard Business Press.

Ulrich, D., Brockbank, W., Yeung, A. K., & Lake, D. G. (1995). Human resource competencies: An empirical assessment. *Human Resource Management, 34*(4), 473–495.

Ulrich, D., Kryscynski, D., Ulrich, M., & Brockbank, W. (2017). Competencies for HR professionals who deliver outcomes. Extracted from https://deepblue.lib.umich.edu/bitstream/handle/2027.42/138377/ert21623.pdf?sequence=1 on 04.01.2020.

Unmanned aerial vehicle. (2019). Extracted from https://en.wikipedia.org/wiki/Unmanned_aerial_vehicle on 07.05.2019.

Uotila, J. (2018). Punctuated equilibrium or ambidexterity: Dynamics of incremental and radical organizational change over time. *Industrial and Corporate Change, 27*(1), 131–148.

US News. (2010). Extracted from https://money.usnews.com/money/blogs/flowchart/2010/08/19/10-great-companies-that-lost-their-edge on 07.05.2019.

Uzunova, P. (2012). HR Competency Model for Competency Management: An Explorative Case Study. (*Thesis, Tilburg University*).

Valentin, E. K. (2001). SWOT analysis from a resource-based view. *Journal of Marketing Theory and Practice, 9*(2), 54–69.

Van Buren, M. E., & Werner, J. M. (1996). High performance work systems. *Business and Economic Review, 43*, 15–35.

Van de Ven, A. H., & Poole, M. S. (1995). Explaining development and change in organizations. *Academy of Management Review, 20*(3), 512.

Van de Ven, A. H., Angle, H. L., & Poole M. (1989). *Research on the Management of Innovation: The Minnesota Studies*. New York: Harper and Row.

Van Nistelrooij, A. T. M. (2018). Coping with uncertainty during change: A relational approach inspired by Kurt Lewin. *Challenging Organisations and Society, 7*(1), 1270–1280.

Varghese, F., Das, V. M., & Jebamalai, V. (2016). Organisational culture-A potential source of organisational commitment. *IPE Journal of Management, 6*(1), 118.

Verma, A. (1995). Employee involvement in the workplace. In M. Gunderson & A. Ponak (Eds.), *Research in Personnel and Human Resource Management*. New Haven, CT: JAI Press.

Victor, B., & Cullen, J. B. (1988). The organizational bases of ethical work climates. *Administrative Science Quarterly, 33*(1), 101–125.

Vocoli. (2014). Extracted from https://www.vocoli.com/blog/july-2014/10-companies-that-failed-to-innovate-and-what-happened-to-them/ on 23.01.2021.

Von Braun, C. F. (1990). The acceleration trap. *MIT Sloan Management Review, 32*(1), 49–55.

Waddell, D., & Sohal, A. S. (1998). Resistance: A constructive tool for change management. *Management Decision, 36*(8), 543–548.

Wagner, A. J. (1994). Participation's effects on performance and satisfaction: A reconsideration of research evidence. *Academy of Management Review, 19*(2), 312–330.

Waiting Line, Outlook Business. (2010). Extracted from http://archive.outlookbusiness.com/printarticle.aspx?266810 on 21.01.2021.

Walker, J. W. (1999). Perspectives: Is HR Ready for the 21st Century?. *Human Resource Planning, 2*(2),5–7.

Walker, J. W., & Stopper, W. G. (2000). Developing human resources leaders. *Human Resource Planning, 23*(1), 38–44.

Wanberg, C. R., & Banas, J. T. (2000). Predictors and outcomes of openness to changes in a reorganizing workplace. *Journal of Applied Psychology*, *85*(1), 132.

Wang, H. (2004). A framework to support and understand strategic decision-making in business to-business electronic commerce. In *The International Workshop on Business and Information*. (BAI2004), Taipei.

Wang, J., Hutchins, H. M., & Garavan, T. N. (2009). Exploring the strategic role of human resource development in organizational crisis management. *Human Resource Development Review*, *8*(1), 22–53.

Wang, B., Liu, Y., & Parker, S. K. (2020). How does the use of information communication technology affect individuals? A work design perspective. *Academy of Management Annals*, *14*(2), 695–725.

Watkins, M. (2003). *The first 90 days: Critical success strategies for new leaders at all levels*. Boston, MA: Harvard Business School Press.

Watkins, M. (2019). *The Three Pillars of Executive On-Boarding*. Talent Management. Extracted from https://ph.drakeintl.com/drakepulse/the-three-pillars-of-executive-onboarding/ on 21.01.2021.

Watson, D., & Clark, L. A. (1997). Extraversion and its positive emotional core. In S. Briggs, W. Jones, & R. Hogan (Eds.), *Handbook of personality psychology* (pp. 767–793). New York: Academic Press.

Weick, K. E. (1993). Organizational Redesign as Improvisation. In G. P. Huber & W. H. Glick, (Eds.), *Organizational Change and Redesign* (pp. 346–379). New York: Oxford University Press.

Weick, K. E., & Quinn, R. E. (1999). Organizational change and development. *Annual Review of Psychology*, *50*(1), 361–386.

Weidenbaum, M. L. (1980). Public policy: No longer a spectator sport for business. *Journal of Business Strategy*, *1*(1), 46–53.

Weisbord, M. R. (1976). Organizational Diagnosis: Six places to look for trouble with or without a theory. *Group and Organization Studies*, *1*(4), 430–447.

Westerman, G., & Bonnet, D. (2015). Revamping your business through digital transformation. *MIT Sloan Management Review*, *56*(3), 10.

Westney, D. E. (1993). Institutionalization theory and the multinational corporation. In S. Ghoshal & E. Westney (Eds.), *Organization Theory and the Multinational Corporation* (pp. 53–76). London: Palgrave Macmillan.

Whelan-Berry, K. S., & Somerville, K. A. (2010). Linking change drivers and the organizational change process: A review and synthesis. *Journal of Change Management*, *10*(2), 175–193.

Whitbourne, S. K. (1986). Openness to experience, identity flexibility, and life change in adults. *Journal of Personality and Social Psychology*, *50*(1), 163–168.

White, K. L. (2001). Revolution for the human spirit. *Organization Development Journal*, *19*(2), 47–58.

Whyte, W. (1956). *The Organization Man*. New York: Simon & Schuster.

Wiersma, E. (2009). For which purposes do managers use Balanced

Scorecards?: An empirical study. *Management Accounting Research*, *20*(4), 239–251.

Wiley, C. (1998). Re-examining perceived ethics issues and ethics roles among employment managers. *Journal of Business Ethics*, *17*(2), 147–161.

Wilkins, A. L., & Ouchi, W. G. (1983). Efficient cultures: Exploring the relationship between culture and organizational performance. *Administrative Science Quarterly*, *28*(3), 468–481.

Williamson, O. E. (2000). The new institutional economics: taking stock, looking ahead. *Journal of Economic Literature*, *38*(3), 595–613.

Wilson, D. C. (1992). *A Strategy of Change: Concepts and Controversies in the Management of Change*. London, UK: Routledge.

Winner, L. (1986). *The Whale and the Reactor: A Search for Limits in an Age of High Technology*. Chicago, IL: University of Chicago Press.

Witcher, B. J., & Chau, V. S. (2010). *Strategic Management Principles and Practice*. United Kingdom: Cengage Learning EMEA.

Wood, S. (1999). Human resource management and performance. *International Journal Of Management Reviews*, *1*(4), 367–413.

Wright, P. M., & McMahan, G. C. (1992). Theoretical perspectives for strategic human resource management. *Journal of Management*, *18*(2), 295–320.

Wright, K. L., &Thompsen, J. A. (1997). Building the people's capacity for change. *The TQM Magazine*, *9*(1), 36–41.

Yager, S. E. (1997). Everything's coming up virtual. *Crossroads*, *4*(1), 20–24.

Yolles, M. (Ed.). (2006). *Organizations as complex systems: An introduction to knowledge cybernetics*. Greenwich, CT: IAP.

Young, T. (2013). Change Management and Defence Administration: Models for Implementing Change. *MBA applied research paper, Athabasca University*.

Yu, D., Zhu, Q., Guo, D., Huang, B., & Su, J. (2015, June). jBPM4S: A multitenant extension of jBPM to support BPaaS. In *Asia-Pacific Conference on Business Process Management* (pp. 43–56). Cham: Springer.

Yukl, G. (1989). Managerial leadership: A review of theory and research. *Journal of Management*, *15*(2), 251–289.

Yukl, G. (2008). *Leadership in Organizations* (7th Ed.). Upper Saddle River, NJ: Prentice Hall.

Zaltman, G., & Duncan, R. (1977). *Strategies for Planned Change*. New York: John Wiley & Sons.

Zaltman, G., Duncan, R., & Holbek, J. (1973). *Innovations and Organizations*. New York: John Wiley & Sons.

Zardkoohi, A. (1985). On the political participation of the firm in the electoral process. *Southern Economic Journal*, *51*(3), 804–817.

Zee, Great Place to Work. (2019). Extracted from https://www.greatplacetowork.in/great/rated/100-best/Zee-Entertainment-Enterprises-Limited on 08.01.2021

Zohar, D., & Marshall, I. (2000). *SQ: Spiritual Intelligence, The Ultimate Intelligence*. New York: Bloomsbury Publishing.

Zula, K. J., & Chermack, T. J. (2007). Integrative literature review: Human capital planning: A review of literature and implications for human resource development. *Human Resource Development Review, 6*(3), 245–262.

Župerkienė, E., Paulikas, J., & Abele, L. (2019, September). Employee behavioural patterns in resisting the implementation of organisational innovation. In *Forum Scientiae Oeconomia 7*(3), 89–100.

Zvirbule, B., & Vilka, I. (2012). Impact of Social Environment on Economic Development in the Baltic States. World Academy of Science, Engineering and Technology, *International Journal of Social, Behavioral, Educational, Economic, Business and Industrial Engineering, 6*(4), 392–395.

Appendix
Comparison of Change Models

	Classification Approach					Hard and Soft Approach			Metaphorical Approach			
Model	Degree of Change	Timing of Change	Scale of Change	Focus of Change	Intentionality	Theory E	Theory O	Theory E & O	Machine	Political System	Organism	Flux or transformation
Kotter, Eight Steps	First/Second	Revolutionary	Modular/Corporate	Structure/Process/Attitude	Planned/Emergent	X	X	X	X	X	X	X
Lewin, Three-Step Model	First/Second	Revolutionary	Modular/Corporate	Structure/Process/Attitude	Planned	X			X		X	
Nadler and Tushman, Congruence Model	Second Order	Revolutionary	Corporate	Structure/Process/Attitude	Planned	X	X	X		X	X	
Peter Senge's Systemic Model	Second Order	Revolutionary	Corporate	Structure/Process/Attitude	Planned/Emergent	X	X	X		X	X	X

Legend

Classification Approach

Degree of Change –
First Order – Minor change.
Second Order – Transformational the entire organization.

Timing of Change –
Revolutionary – Sudden and drastic.
Evolutionary – Gradual and incremental.

Scale of Change –
Fine Tuning – Ongoing, matching strategy, processes, people, and structure.
Incremental – Modification to strategies and processes.
Modular – Department or divisional level change.
Corporate – Radical change to business strategy.

Hard and soft Approach

Theory E – Change initiated by economic value. Hard changes: downsizing, restructure.
Theory O – Change initiated by organizational capability. Soft changes: develop culture, individual and org. learning.
Theory E & O – Hard change first followed by soft changes later.

Metaphorical Approach

Machine – Change by those in a position of authority. Resistance to change must be managed. Change must be well planned and

Political – System – Change must be supported by a powerful person. The wider the support base the better. Understand who will be the winners and losers. Creating new coalitions and renegotiating

Organism – Change is made in response to the external environment. Individuals need to be aware of the need for change. The response to change can be designed and worked towards.

Focus of Change –		
Structure –	Altering the org. chart, reward system, or policies and procedures.	Participation and psychological support needed to succeed.
Process –	Altering the way people interact within structures.	
Attitude –	How people feel about working within existing structures and processes.	
Intentionality –		
Planned –	Planned – Intentional change with a strategy and expertise. It is linear.	
Emergent –	Emergent – Change is seen as process, driven from the bottom-up.	
		Flux and Transformati-on – Change emerges; it is not managed. Managers are a part of the whole environment. Tensions and conflict are a key feature of emerging change. Managers act as enablers.

Methods of Cataloguing Change Models. Source: Adapted from Young (2013). Applied Research Project on "Change Management and Defence Administration: Models for Implementing Change", Athabasca University.

Index

Printed in the United States
by Baker & Taylor Publisher Services